Home to

HARMONY

Home to
HARMONY

Philip Gulley

Multnomah® Publishers *Sisters, Oregon*

HOME TO HARMONY
published by Multnomah Publishers, Inc.
Copyright © 2000 by Philip Gulley
International Standard Book Number: 1-57673-613-X

Cover illustration by Robin Moline/Conrad Represents
Cover design by The Office of Bill Chiaravalle
Interior map illustration by Mike Wepplo

Scripture quotations are from the *Revised Standard Version Bible* (RSV)
© 1946, 1952 by the Division of Christian Education of the National Council of the
Churches of Christ in the United States of America

Multnomah is a trademark of Multnomah Publishers, Inc.,
and is registered in the U.S. Patent and Trademark Office.
The colophon is a trademark of Multnomah Publishers, Inc.

Printed in the United States of America

FOR INFORMATION:
MULTNOMAH PUBLISHERS, INC.•POST OFFICE BOX 1720•SISTERS, OREGON 97759

Library of Congress Cataloging-in-Publication Data:
Gulley, Philip.
Home to harmony/by Philip Gulley.
    p. cm.—(Harmony series; bk 1)
ISBN 1-57673-613-X
1. City and town life—Fiction. 2. Quakers—Fiction. 3. Clergy—Fiction. I. Title.
PS3557.U449 H66 2000
813'.54—dc21
    00-008520

00 01 02 03 04 05 06 07—10 9 8 7 6 5 4 3 2 1

*This book is dedicated to my wife Joan, who,
after two children and sixteen years of marriage, delights me still.*

*It is dedicated also to the memory of Nancy Mullen,
whose strong Quaker spirit was a blessing to all who knew her.*

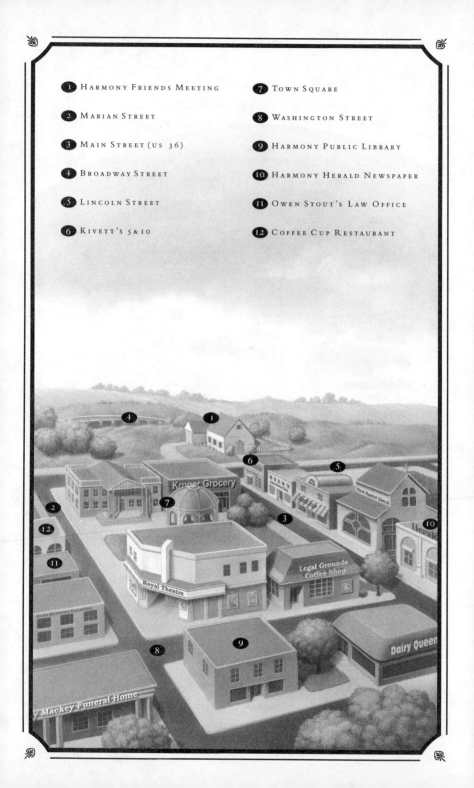

1. HARMONY FRIENDS MEETING

2. MARIAN STREET

3. MAIN STREET (US 36)

4. BROADWAY STREET

5. LINCOLN STREET

6. KIVETT'S 5 & 10

7. TOWN SQUARE

8. WASHINGTON STREET

9. HARMONY PUBLIC LIBRARY

10. HARMONY HERALD NEWSPAPER

11. OWEN STOUT'S LAW OFFICE

12. COFFEE CUP RESTAURANT

Contents

Map of Harmony 6

Spring

1. *Home to Harmony* 11
2. *Settling In* 19
3. *The Bobservation Post* 27
4. *The Swordfish* 35
5. *Revival* 43
6. *Uly* 51

Summer

7. *Miss Rudy, Wilbur, and Friday Nights* 63
8. *Burma-Shave* 71
9. *The Birds and the Bees* 79
10. *This Callous Pride* 87
11. *The Aluminum Years* 95
12. *Brother Norman and the Bus* 103

Fall

13. *First Grade* 115
14. *Noodle Day* 123
15. *The World* 129
16. *Mutiny* 135
17. *The Twins* 145
18. *Roger and Tiffany* 155

Winter

19. *Miriam and Ellis* 165
20. *Memory* 173
21. *The Spelling Bee* 179
22. *The Testimony* 191
23. *Legal Grounds* 203
24. *The Shroud of Harmony* 213

Note to the Reader

This book is a work of fiction. Any similarities between persons in this book and real persons are strictly coincidental. Except that I know a man who is every bit as aggravating as Dale Hinshaw.

Certain historians maintain that Ulysses S. Grant II never moved to Harmony, never married a Quaker, and never opened a hardware store. Everyone is entitled to their opinion.

"The Bobservation Post" was a cherished staple of *The Danville Gazette* and was the brainchild of its distinguished editor, Mr. Robert Pearcy.

Philip Gulley

Spring

One

Home to Harmony

hen I was in the second grade, my teacher, Miss Maxwell, read from *The Harmony Herald* that one in every four children lived in China. I remember looking over the room, guessing which children they might be. I wasn't sure where China was, but suspected it was on bus route three. I recall being grateful I didn't live in China because I didn't care for Chinese food and couldn't speak the language.

I liked living where I did, in Harmony. I liked that the Dairy Queen sold ice cream cones for a dime. I liked that I could ride my Schwinn Typhoon there without crossing Main Street, which my mother didn't allow.

I liked that I lived four blocks from the Kroger grocery store, where every spring they stacked bags of peat moss out front. My brother and I would climb on the bags and vault from stack to stack. Once, on a particularly high leap, my brother hit the *K* in *KROGER* with his head, causing the neon tube to shatter. For the next year, the sign flashed *ROGER*, which we considered an amazing coincidence since that was my brother's name. He liked to pass by at night and see his name in lights.

I liked that we had no curfew and after a certain age could wander anywhere in town we pleased. My parents were not lax; this was the usual order of things in our town. Harmony presented so few temptations that it took a resourceful person to find trouble, and we were not that clever. This was a burden to us. We wanted to wreak havoc and be feared as hoodlums, but the town would not cooperate.

Most of all, I liked that Harmony sat on Highway 36, which began in Roanoke, Ohio, near the Cy Young Memorial and ran west through Indiana, Illinois, Missouri, and Kansas to Commanche Crossing, Colorado. There was a map at the Rexall drugstore which showed all the towns along Highway 36 with a gold star stuck on Harmony. Most folks don't know about us because when you open the Rand McNally map to our state we're hidden underneath the left staple. That's fine with us. We're modest people, inclined to shun attention.

On summer days I would sit on the bench in front of the Rexall and eat Milk Duds and watch the license plates. Then I would pedal home and eat Sugar Pops cereal down to the bottom of the box, to the *free license plate in every box!* I would reach down, pluck out that license plate, blow the sugar off, then hang it from my bicycle seat and pretend I was from Rhode Island or Arizona or wherever the license plate dictated.

But pretending was as far as it went. I never wanted to live anywhere but Harmony. When I went away to college and other students asked me where I wanted to live after school, I would tell them Harmony. They said I lacked ambition, which wasn't true. They confused contentment for stagnation, a common mistake. Even at that young age I knew contentment was a rare gift and saw no need to seek it elsewhere when I had found it in Harmony.

On my first Sunday back after college, Dale Hinshaw, an elder of the

Harmony Friends Meeting, asked me what I was going to do with my life. I had given considerable thought to that question but hadn't reached any conclusions. I told Dale I wasn't sure, but when I found out I'd be sure to let him know.

That was when Dale prophesied that God was calling me to the ministry.

"Sam Gardner," he declared, "the fields are ripe for harvest. Go ye into the fields."

I took him seriously, for Dale Hinshaw was rumored to be wise, though I would learn later that rumors of his wisdom were circulated only by persons who did not know him well.

I went to seminary, despite Dale's warning that theological training would be my undoing. He said, "You don't want to go there. That's a nest of atheists at that school. They talk about God being dead. Boy, won't they be surprised."

According to Dale, God was going to surprise a lot of people.

But I went to seminary anyway, graduated after four years, then took a church in the next state over where I pastored twelve years before leaving for health reasons: I was sick of them and they were sick of me.

I had met my wife in college. Her name was Barbara, and she was the first woman besides my mother to show the faintest interest in me. It took six years to persuade her to marry me. What I lacked in charm I made up for in persistence, and I finally wore her down. We had two sons, Levi and Addison.

Now I was taking my family to live with my parents in Harmony. I was sorely depressed. Thirty-eight years old, married with two children, and living with my parents.

I began praying God would provide a job. I prayed every day. I wasn't picky—any job would do. In the thick of my prayers, Pastor Taylor of Harmony Friends Meeting died. Both his parents had died of heart problems, which he feared would happen to him, so he'd begun to jog and was hit by a truck. This was not the answer to prayer I had envisioned, and I went to Pastor Taylor's funeral burdened with guilt.

He was buried the week before Easter. The church held a meeting to decide what to do. Fern Hampton, president of the Friendly Women's Circle, seemed less concerned with Pastor Taylor's death and more concerned with his poor timing.

"For a minister, that was pretty inconsiderate of him to go and get killed during Lent," she said.

Then she suggested I bring the Easter message. "You can do it, Sam," she said. "Besides, we're desperate."

*I*t being Easter, I preached on the Resurrection. I told how in the resurrection of Jesus, God rejected our rejection. In the crucifixion we said no to God, but in the resurrection God said yes to us. I told them that God covets every lost soul.

"It's not God's will that any should perish," I declared. Then I told of the good shepherd who searched until every sheep was found, of the forgiving father who ran to embrace his straying son.

It was grace-full preaching. I even pounded the pulpit. Twice. Many pulpits have been pounded in the name of hellfire; I thought it was time to pound one in the name of grace.

Fern Hampton sat in the sixth row, her face pruned up. This was not the gospel she had learned as a child. She was not a big believer in grace. As theories go, grace was good, but in reality it lacked satisfaction. Fern was a disciple of retribution. In her opinion, Jesus was a bit too quick to forgive. She wanted God to punish sinners and had strong opinions about with whom He should start.

After worship, I stood at the meetinghouse door greeting people and shaking hands. Men with shirts buttoned to the top, neck fat spilling over their collars. Ladies in flowered dresses, bathed in perfume and heavy with Easter corsages. Children running amongst their tree trunk legs, just as I had when I was their age. Fern Hampton was the last person through. She eyed me up and down for a moment, then asked, "Wherever did you learn such foolishness?"

This is how foreign grace was to her, that when she heard it she mistook it for heresy. There are some people, I am sorry to say, who wouldn't recognize grace if it stood at their door wearing a name tag.

That night the phone rang at my parents' house. It was Harvey Muldock, who sold cars for a living and was in charge of the pastoral search committee. Harvey got the job because he was on vacation when the committee was formed and wasn't there to defend himself. His first Sunday back, he opened the bulletin and there was the announcement thanking him for volunteering: *Harvey Muldock will lead our search for a new pastor. Thank you, Harvey, for your willingness to serve.* This was how many of the church jobs were filled, causing some members to swear off vacations altogether.

Harvey asked if I would serve as the new pastor of Harmony Friends Meeting.

I told him I would need to pray about it. Harvey, being a car dealer, thought I was merely driving a hard bargain. He offered to throw in two weeks' vacation and a new Plymouth at invoice price.

During the next week I prayed for a sign, preferably a dramatic one—words in the sky or a voice in my dreams. Once I even closed my eyes, opened my Bible, and dropped my finger onto a passage to see if it might hold God's answer. I had read stories of people doing this and finding just the answer they needed. I know a man, who, when faced with the question of whether he should be a pastor, landed his finger directly on Matthew 28:19: "Go therefore and make disciples of all nations..."

Hoping for a similar affirmation, I closed my eyes, opened my Bible, and plunked my finger down on Romans 4:11—a verse concerning

Abraham's circumcision. It made me wince, but offered little insight.

I called Harvey to tell him I was still praying. He offered a free automatic transmission and three weeks' vacation. Then he mentioned that the job would pay enough for me to buy my own house, and at that moment God's will for my life became abundantly clear. I confess I also felt somewhat responsible for Pastor Taylor's demise and felt obligated to fill the void his passing created.

I told Harvey I would be pleased to speak God's grace to the people of Harmony Friends.

Looking back, I'm not sure that's what they had in mind. I think they were wanting someone to open the church doors, shovel the walk, and mow the grass. I did all those things, then threw in grace for good measure.

Sometimes what we think we need isn't what we need at all, and what gets thrown in for good measure is that which fills our hearts.

*T*he bench still sits in front of the Rexall. Sometimes I eat my lunch there and watch the license plates and wonder about the passing people—where they've been and where they're headed. I thought I knew them, but now that I'm their pastor it occurs to me that I don't know them at all. Perhaps I never did. Never knew their desolations, their pinings, their hunger for grace in a grace-starved world. The only things I know of them are the things they want me to know.

We share this corner of the world, huddled together on Highway 36—the Rexall, Harvey Muldock's car dealership, the meetinghouse, the Grant Hardware Emporium, and the Dairy Queen under whose lights the moths still dance on July evenings. This is the stage where our dappled lives unfold.

When I was away at college, a sociology professor talked to us about

"anomie." He said anomie is when you lack roots, when you feel you don't belong.

In this anomie world, Harmony is a strong comfort to me. I sit on the Rexall bench and my roots grow down and hold me fast. Some folks find their joy in wandering, but I found mine in coming home.

At Pastor Taylor's funeral we sang his favorite hymn, "Softly and Tenderly." We reached the chorus. The women sang high, the men low.

> *Come home, come home,*
> *ye who are weary, come home.*

We sang that song and wept and then settled Pastor Taylor in Johnny Mackey's hearse for the procession to Mill Creek Cemetery. It was a beautiful spring morning. A fine day for travel, for going home. Visibility good with the wind to his back. We took up the ropes, lowered him in the grave, and prayed him Godspeed.

And that is how Pastor Taylor went home to his harmony, and I came home to mine.

Two

Settling In

The first time I met Dr. Neely was the day he pulled me into the world.

Though I've tried hard to recall that meeting, it has escaped me. So my first memory of him is when I was five years old and needed my polio shot for first grade. I remember sitting in his waiting room smelling the antiseptic, while my mother read to me from *Highlights* magazine about the Timbertoes family—Ma and Pa, the Timbertoes' children, Tommy and Mabel, and the Timbertoes' goat, Butter.

Butter had eaten Tommy's report card, to Tommy's great relief. He had flunked spelling and with his report card gone was now free to embellish his academic record. Except that Ma and Pa found out, gave Tommy a spanking, and sent him to his room. It made me leery of education: First you get jabbed with a needle, then you get spanked.

I was meditating on the perils of education when the nurse called out, "Sam Gardner." My mother said, "That's you," and lifted me off her lap. We followed the nurse down the hallway to Dr. Neely's office. He was sitting on a round stool. He patted the table next to him and said, "Hop up here, Tiger," which thrilled me.

Tiger! I had often thought myself as tigerlike. Strong and sleek and primed for the kill. I liked hiding in the forsythia bush next to the porch and yelling out my brother's name, then pouncing on him as he walked past. Yes, a tiger. I marveled at Dr. Neely's perception. Which is why I remember that day and have thought fondly of him ever since. Even when I dropped my britches and he stuck me with a needle, I still liked him.

He's still my doctor, though he's nearly eighty and no longer keeps abreast of the latest medical breakthroughs. Dr. Neely doesn't like pills. He likes to give shots, right in the rear, where the good Lord put the padding. Pills are too easy. If all people have to do is take a pill, they'll bother him with the least little ailment. But if they have to get a shot, they think twice about bothering him. Dr. Neely's theory is that if you're not willing to get poked with a needle, then you're probably not sick enough to see a doctor.

He's been the only doctor in Harmony for fifty years and knows every bottom in town. He maintains that bottoms are like fingerprints—no two are alike. In 1973, when Roger Morgan died in a car wreck down in the city, Dr. Neely identified him at the morgue by his buttocks. He told about it at the Coffee Cup afterwards. The coroner pulled back the sheet and Dr. Neely said, "Yep, that's Roger Morgan. I'd know those cheeks anywhere. That's the Morgan dimple."

*D*r. Neely and his wife moved to our town after the Big War back in 1946. They bought a house on Washington Street, three blocks south of the Grant Hardware Emporium. They had three children—two daughters and a little boy named Jack, who died of leukemia at the age of seven. They buried little Jack in the Mill Creek Cemetery west of town. Every Sunday since, they have driven to the cemetery and placed a little toy car on Jack's grave. Their little boy loved toy cars. Even when he was sick, he'd lie in the hospital and pretend his legs were mountains and the blanket wrinkles were the roads, pushing the car up the mountains and down the roads while he made engine noises.

It was horrible to be a doctor and not be able to heal your own child. Dr. Neely sat next to his son's bed and watched his skin turn yellow and listened to his gasping breath, then saw Jack's tiny body shudder and his hand let loose of the toy car. He tries not to think of it. Except every now and then, late at night, when the house is quiet and sleep won't come, he sits at his desk, holds that very toy car, and thinks back.

Every Saturday, Dr. Neely stops by Kivett's Five and Dime on his way home and buys a toy car. The cashiers thought he was giving them to the children at his office. He has a drawer of toys. If you don't cry when he gives you a shot, he'll pull open the drawer and let you reach in and pick out a toy. The cashiers at the Five and Dime thought that's why he bought a toy car every Saturday. But if they had passed by Mill Creek Cemetery on Sundays after dinner, they'd have known otherwise.

Shortly after I was hired as the pastor of Harmony Friends, my wife and I were walking past the Neely home one Saturday afternoon. Our boys were tagging behind us. Dr. Neely's garage door was open, and we could see him at his workbench painting a For Sale sign. We stopped to visit.

The Neelys were selling their house. It was too big, and they were too old. They were selling it themselves, having worn out three realtors. The Neelys were only willing to sell their house to someone who would agree not to paint the wall behind the dining room draperies. It was the wall where their children's heights had been recorded as they had grown.

Back when the Neely kids were little, their names were written in Mrs. Neely's careful printing. As soon as they learned to write their own names, she'd have them do it. The first day of every year, they'd mark their heights and write their names.

The Neelys hadn't given it much thought, until a lady wanting to buy the house talked about wallpapering the dining room and they pulled back the draperies to show her the names.

"You can't wallpaper in here. It'll cover the names," Mrs. Neely had told her. Jack's name was there, to the right of the forty-two-inch mark. A capital *J* leaning to the left. A small *a*. A backwards *c* and a capital *K*. Now there was a stranger in their dining room talking about covering it over.

Dr. Neely took the lady gently by the arm, led her to the door, and thanked her for her interest. No sale. Now they were looking for someone to buy the house who wouldn't cover their children's names.

"Some people don't respect things like that," Dr. Neely told us as he sat at his workbench. "They think buying a house gives them the right to do with it as they please, with no regard for anything."

My wife told him she'd never cover over a child's name.

Dr. Neely continued, "It's just that every now and then if I were walking past, I'd want to be able to sit on the porch or maybe come inside and see Jack's name. Just knowing I could do that would help a lot."

We told him we understood.

*I*t was a wonderful house. When my brother and I were little and would trick-or-treat there, Mrs. Neely would usher us into the entryway. As she dropped a popcorn ball in my sack, I'd marvel at their house. It had a front porch and a sleeping porch on the second floor and oak trees and ivy up the chimney and stone sidewalks with moss between the stones. It had a kitchen, dining room, two parlors, a den with a fireplace, two bathrooms plus a shower in the basement, four bedrooms, an attic, and a basement. And a garage with a workbench.

The Neely house was built back when house plans were rough ideas in a carpenter's head. There were the usual rooms, with a few extra rooms added for good measure. What you did with those rooms was your own business. If you wanted to put books in the dining room and call it a study, the architect didn't throw a fit because there was no architect. There was just a carpenter and the man he hired to help him.

few weeks later I took my oldest son, Levi, to Dr. Neely for his first-grade shots. Levi and I sat in the waiting room reading about the Timbertoes family. Tommy had forgotten to do his homework, so he told his teacher that Butter the goat had eaten his computer disk. She didn't believe him, but didn't say so for fear of hurting Tommy's self-esteem. She did call Pa Timbertoes to tell him. Thirty-some years later, Pa is a reformed spanker. No more spankings. Instead, he sent Tommy to a therapist. Modern education seems a far safer prospect than when I was a child.

Then the nurse called out "Levi Gardner," and I said, "That's you," and we walked down the hallway to Dr. Neely's office where he called Levi "Tiger," poked his bottom with a needle, then opened the drawer and let him pick a toy.

I asked Dr. Neely if he'd sold his house yet.

"Nope. Some fella come to look at it. He talked about ripping out the wall between the kitchen and dining room to make a culinary suite. What in the world is a culinary suite? He kept waving his arms around, talking about opening the space up and letting it breathe."

I told Dr. Neely I'd never knock down a wall in a house as grand as his.

He asked me where we were living. I told him we were staying with my folks but looking for a place to buy.

He said, "Sam, why don't you and Barbara buy our house?"

I told him we couldn't afford it on a Quaker pastor's salary.

He peered over his glasses at me. "Too bad the Lord didn't call you to the Episcopalian ministry," he said.

That night after supper the phone rang. It was Dr. Neely calling to see if Barbara and I could come over; he and Mrs. Neely had something to ask us.

When we walked up their sidewalk, the Neelys were sitting on their front porch drinking iced tea. Mrs. Neely offered us a glass. We sat in the swing, a gentle swaying back and forth, the glasses sweating in our hands.

Dr. Neely cleared his throat. "Sam and Barbara, we think a great deal of you. We'd like to sell you our house."

I started to tell Dr. Neely we couldn't afford it, but he raised his hand. "Hear me out," he said.

"The house is worth a hundred and fifty thousand. We'll sell it to you for a hundred thousand if you agree not to cover over the names in the dining room or tear down any walls. And every now and then, we might want to come visit. Plus, on Saturday mornings, I'd like to bring my newspaper and read it on the porch. Would that be all right with you?"

It was.

So they moved out and we moved in. Every Saturday morning, weather permitting, Dr. Neely brings his paper and sits reading it in his old porch rocker. And every now and again, they stop in to visit and pull aside the dining room curtain and remember. Mrs. Neely will reach out and trace her finger along Jack's name. Over the left-leaning *J* and the small *a* and the backward *c* and the capital *K*.

Our first week in the house, I took my boys and stood them along the wall on the other side of the dining room window and marked their heights. Levi wrote his name in crooked kindergarten letters. Six inches underneath it, I wrote Addison's name and the date.

People ask us where we live. We tell them the old Neely house three blocks south of the Grant Hardware Emporium. I don't know how long it will take before it becomes the old Gardner place, but I'm in no hurry. In Harmony, having a house named for you is not a privilege conferred by mere ownership. Status isn't for sale in this town; it is earned.

Our first night in the house, my wife and I were lying in bed. I was thanking God for my blessings. Thanking God for not having to pull aside a dining room curtain to have my children near—that they were right down the hall, asleep in their Superman underwear, their little chests rising and falling to the pulse of their dreams.

I thought how some blessings are fickle guests. Just when we think they're here to stay, they pack their bags and move. When we're in the midst of blessing, we think it's our due—that blessing lasts forever. Next thing you know we're sitting helpless beside a hospital bed. All we're left with is a name on a wall, a toy in a desk, and memories that haunt our sleep.

Sometimes we come to gratitude too late. It's only after blessing has passed on that we realize what we had.

When Mrs. Neely stands in our dining room, tracing her finger along the names, I bet that's what she's thinking—that the time to delight in blessing is when blessing is close at hand.

Three

The Bobservation Post

The summer of my eighteenth year, my grandfather died and I inherited his chest of drawers. I wanted to inherit his gentle disposition, but had to settle for his chest of drawers. When I left for college I took it with me. After college I hauled it from one apartment to another, then to a parsonage. Now it is back in the town from whence it came, settled in between the windows of our bedroom. I hope never to move it again.

When I open it to pull out clean underwear, I think back to when I was little and would visit my grandparents. I'd walk the three blocks to their house and through the wood screen door and there would be my grandparents, waiting for me. We'd eat lunch at the table my grandfather had built, then my grandfather and I would go to his workshop and build birdhouses.

Three o'clock was the time for our naps. I would lie on the couch and my grandparents would doze on their twin beds. When I could hear my grandfather snore and knew he was asleep, I would pull a chair up to his chest of drawers and rummage through it, searching for treasure—old letters, cuff links, a pocketknife from the 1939 World's Fair in New

York City, and a picture of a woman wearing a swimsuit. The picture was in a little box with Private written on it, which was the only encouragement I needed to open the box for inspection.

In the bottom drawer, underneath his long underwear, were brittle clippings from *The Harmony Herald* chronicling our family history. There was an article describing my grandparents' wedding and their honeymoon plans: an overnight trip to the Statler Hotel in the city. One room, breakfast included, for $9.50. My grandfather paper clipped the receipt to the newspaper article.

Uncle Addison was born nine months and one day later. He was the first of four children and the most popular boy in town. He was captain of the football team and voted most likely to move away. At his high school graduation, the principal prophesied that Uncle Addison would be a senator someday, maybe even president. He won a scholarship to college, then a month before he was to go he died in a car wreck. His obituary was also in the bottom drawer, folded inside his first report card.

My grandparents rarely spoke of him, for the pain of it. But when I was born, my mother named me for her brother—Samuel Addison. It was a dreadful burden to be named for a dead man, for the longer he was dead the greater he became. It limited my freedom. There was pressure to be like him. I was five years old and people asked what I wanted to be when I grew up. I told them I wanted to be a cowboy and they looked away in grim disappointment. Except for my grandfather, who told me the world could always use a good cowboy.

My grandfather also kept newspaper pictures of me and my brother Roger, photos published the weeks we were born—a *Herald* tradition which continues to this day. Children born to a Harmony family get their pictures in the paper. Each week, Bob Miles Jr., editor of the *Herald,* fills the paper with pictures and articles of people in our town in the hope they'll buy extra copies and mail them to relatives. Human pride being what it is, we do just that.

The Harmony Herald is delivered free on Friday afternoons to every house and business in town. People read it, but not for the news, which we already know. We read the *Herald* to see if our names are in it. We scan the society column written by Bob's wife, Arvella, to see if we're mentioned. We thumb over to the school news to see whose children made the honor roll. Then we turn to the church news to see what the pastor of the Baptist church is going to preach about that Sunday.

If our names are in the paper, we buy extra copies to send to our relatives. This is how Bob Jr. makes his living, selling extra copies. That, and out-of-town subscriptions. People who grew up here and moved to the city pay thirty dollars a year to remember why they left town in the first place.

Like any town, there are those who can't wait to move from here.

"To heck with them," Dale Hinshaw says. "We're better off without them. Let 'em move to the city and forget their heritage. They'll be sorry."

When they come back to town to visit, they don't seem sorry. They look like they're having a good time in the city. They come home for Thanksgiving and stay only as long as etiquette requires. This town isn't for everyone. Just because we like it doesn't mean it's the only place worth living. Being grateful for what you have doesn't give you the right to tear down the choices other people have made. If the city makes them happy, I'm glad for them.

We live in Harmony because we want to be here. Except for Bob Jr., who wishes he had moved away.

When Bob Miles Jr. was a child and the phone rang, his mother would hurry to the kitchen to answer it. She'd stand on her tiptoes and speak into the mouthpiece mounted on the wall, holding the receiver to her ear.

She'd shout hello into the black box. The caller would ask for Bob.

"Bob senior or Bob junior?" she'd clarify. That is how Bob Jr. got his name.

Bob is the fourth Bob in a row in his family. He didn't want to be a Bob, and he didn't want to run *The Harmony Herald*. Bob Jr. wanted to be a foreign correspondent. He has a map of the world on his office wall and a shortwave radio tuned to the BBC. Every evening at eight o'clock he sits in front of the map, puts on his headphones, and listens to the BBC. He dreams of living in Paris. He dreams of war breaking out and the news anchor saying, "Now let's go to Bob Miles, our foreign correspondent, for a firsthand look at this crisis."

Sometimes, when he's all alone, Bob Jr. practices speaking with a British accent, just like the man on the radio.

He stayed home to take over the *Herald* from his father. Bob Jr. writes about the county fair and church news, eats lunch at the Coffee Cup, and is treasurer for the Optimist Club. But underneath that ordinary existence is fixed that remarkable dream.

*N*ot many people know Bob Jr.'s dream. It's not the kind of thing you talk about in this town, lest people think you're uppity for wanting more than Harmony has to offer. If you have aspirations of greatness, you keep them to yourself. The only reason I know Bob's dream is that when I was asked to be the pastor of Harmony Friends, he was the only one to discourage me.

He told me there was a whole world out there, and advised me not to make the mistake he'd made. "There's so much more than this little town," he said. "Don't get stuck here, Sam. You'll shrivel up."

Bob Jr. said it with some bitterness. He's a disillusioned man, and it's partly our fault. We are too sensitive and are too easily offended when he writes the truth about us. The truth is stifled in this town. The right to say what we want, work where we want, live where we want, and worship where we want are not inalienable rights in Harmony. We are chained by expectations. Bob Jr. runs the paper because his father, Bob Sr., ran the paper. Bob Sr. inherited the job from his father, Bob Two, who inherited it from the man who started it all, Bob One. This ruled out Bob Jr. becoming a foreign correspondent and living in a flat in Paris.

Bob Jr.'s father is eighty-two years old and a member of the John Birch Society. He phones every week to complain about Bob Jr.'s editorials. Bob Sr.'s editorials used to routinely call for the summary execution of Communists, foreign spies, and certain Democrats. Bob Jr. writes editorials about recycling and the proliferation of billboards. He is a grim disappointment to his father, who wants him to warn against Chinese aggression, Mexican immigration, and certain Harmony town board members who have sold out to the Mafia. Instead, Bob Jr. writes about the high school graduation and Corn and Sausage Days and three sure-fire ways to increase your tomato yield.

When Bob Jr. was new to the trade, he took the job seriously. He once attended a town board meeting, tape recorded the proceedings, and published it word for word in the *Herald*. This stirred up considerable wrath. It was then he discovered that people weren't interested in truth as much as they were interested in having their prejudices confirmed. So Bob decided to get out of the news business and confine his reporting to weddings, graduations, church happenings, and gardening. A doomsday cult could poison the New York City water supply and kill a million people, and Bob would write about Bea Majors having Sunday dinner at her sister Opal's house.

It's a matter of knowing your readership. Bea Majors visiting her sister's house was big news since they hadn't spoken in twenty years after Opal laid claim to their mother's dining room furniture the day after their mother was buried. But now they've forgiven each other and are back to talking. We don't know anyone in New York City, but we do know Bea and Opal, which makes their reconciliation newsworthy.

It requires a good memory to live in a small town. You have to remember who isn't talking to whom and why, and who's on whose side. If you publish the newspaper and make a favorable comment about Opal Majors's cucumbers, you need to balance it by mentioning Bea's work in the church. Otherwise there'll be letters to the editor condemning your blatant bias and ending with the declaration, "Your newspaper no longer speaks for the majority of right-minded citizens. It is therefore with great sadness that I must cancel my subscription." The fact that the paper is free seems to escape these people.

The most controversial column in the *Herald* is "The Bobservation Post." The *Herald* office sits on the town square. Bob Jr.'s great-grandfather's desk is stationed at the front window. Bob Jr. thought it might interest his readers to learn what he sees from his window, so every Tuesday he sits at that desk, gazes out the office window, and writes his on-the-scene report, "The Bobservation Post."

The first Tuesday he looked out his window to see Fern Hampton walking into the bank during school hours. Fern had left her students with a student teacher for the few minutes it would take to go to the bank. She thought she could get away with it, and probably would have if Bob Jr. hadn't noticed her and mentioned it in his column. Fern almost lost her job and didn't speak to Bob Jr. for two years, which, according to Bob, was not altogether unpleasant.

You learn over the years that if you have any private business to conduct on the town square, you don't do it on Tuesday. If you're a married couple and you visit the attorney, Owen Stout, to draw up a will, you don't go on Tuesday. Otherwise, Bob Jr. will write in "The Bobservation Post" that he saw you visiting Owen's office and people will suspect the worse—that your marriage of thirty years has come to an end, or you've been sued, or you've been arrested for selling drugs and are seeking legal assistance.

When "The Bobservation Post" first came out, it caused much concern and several sharply worded letters to the editor.

"What is happening in this country, when a man can't even walk down Main Street without being spied on?"

"Big Brother is alive and well in Harmony!"

"Your newspaper no longer speaks for the majority of right-minded citizens. It is therefore with great sadness that I must cancel my subscription."

Bob Jr. didn't blink. He printed the First Amendment on the front page of the *Herald*. In capital letters.

CONGRESS SHALL MAKE NO LAW RESPECTING AN ESTABLISHMENT OF RELIGION OR PROHIBITING THE FREE EXERCISE THEREOF; OR ABRIDGING THE FREEDOM OF SPEECH, OR OF THE PRESS; OR THE RIGHT OF THE PEOPLE PEACEABLY TO ASSEMBLE, AND TO PETITION THE GOVERNMENT FOR A REDRESS OF GRIEVANCES.

Then Bob Jr. wrote an editorial in which he declared, "This town is full of people who stand up on Sunday morning to thank God for their freedom, then get upset when anyone exercises it."

Bob Sr. called him on the phone and accused him of being a mouthpiece for the Communists. He asked where he'd learned such nonsense.

"The Constitution," Bob Jr. said. "You ought to read it. There's all kinds of good ideas in there." Then he hung up the phone, something he'd always wanted to do.

There's anger in Bob Jr. and deep cynicism. I can sense it. I'm a little worried about him. It is a burden to spend your life in one place, thinking you'd be happier somewhere else. I pass by his office in the evening and see him in there, staring at his map, listening to the BBC, and feeling trapped. He wants to get away but suspects he never will, that the time for escape has passed.

Once I was hiking through the woods and came upon a fox seized in a trap. The fox had struggled to escape, then had given up and settled in to die. That's the feeling I have about Bob Jr.

I wish he could see the marvel of this place. I wish Harmony brought him the joy it brings me. But there he sits, night after night, pining for Paris. There's danger in thinking joy is a matter of location. If we can't find joy where we are, we probably won't find it anywhere.

My grandfather taught me that. He didn't mean to. It just happened. I was a little boy and amid the symphony of his snores, I'd pull a chair up to his chest of drawers and rummage through it. I'd read the *Herald* clippings and finger the pictures and know I was holding onto happiness.

The leaves of our blessed lives fall to the ground and if we're wise like my grandfather, we gather them in a pile and keep them safe lest the winds of forgetfulness blow them away.

four

The Swordfish

There are two restaurants in Harmony: the McDonald's out on the highway where traveling salesmen stop on their way to the city, and the Coffee Cup, where the rest of us eat when our wives are mad and won't cook.

The Coffee Cup sits on the town square and has ever since 1963, when Vinny Toricelli and his wife, Penny, moved here from the East somewhere. We're not sure where; they've never said. Although we're eager to know the details, Vinny and Penny have never offered any, so we remain in a cloud of unknowing.

Their first ten years here, the town was rife with speculation about their arrival. Some theorized they were in trouble with the law, so changed their names and moved here to avoid arrest. Others said they had abandoned their families to run off together. Dale Hinshaw thought they were in the witness protection program. He conjectured that Vinny, being Italian, had been a hitman for the Mafia and had testified in court in exchange for protection.

It is true that when the Coffee Cup opened a buffet, Bob Miles Jr. wanted to run a picture of Vinny and his buffet in the *Herald* and Vinny refused to have his picture taken. So Bob settled for a picture of the buffet table, with a painting of the Last Supper hanging on the wall behind the buffet. Jesus and His disciples gazing upon iceberg lettuce, sunflower seeds, bacon bits, and four styles of dressing. Vinny added a fifth dressing, Russian, but removed it after accusations of being a Communist sympathizer.

Dale Hinshaw said at the time, "The people in the witness protection program can pick anywhere in the United States to live. The government'll set 'em up in business and even buy them a house. It's a pretty sweet deal, but you have to kill someone to get it."

Bob Jr. grumped, "If they could've lived anywhere, why in the world would they pick this place?"

After a while Vinny and Penny became part of the landscape and we stopped guessing what had brought them here.

Now we're just grateful they're here. Otherwise we'd have to drink our coffee at McDonald's from a Styrofoam cup and burn our lips. Instead, we sit in a booth at the Coffee Cup and drink fresh coffee from mugs that have our names printed on the bottom and that hang on the wall next to the front door when we're not there. We walk in, the bell over the door tinkles, Vinny greets us by name, and we pluck our mugs from the rack and head to our booth—where Penny smiles and pours coffee and hands us menus, even though we know what we want.

*T*he Coffee Cup is long and narrow. There are twelve red vinyl stools at the counter, six red vinyl booths along the wall, and a liar's table at the rear, underneath the stuffed swordfish Vinny brought with him from back East. My parents remember the day Vinny and Penny drove into town in a 1959 Chevrolet with the swordfish tied on top. You don't see that every day and it has stuck in our memories. I meet my father for a cup of coffee and he looks at the fish and asks, "Did

I ever tell you about the first time I saw that fish?" I always say no because it pleases him to tell the story, which he does in detail, right down to the color of the car (light blue with a cream top); the weather (mostly sunny with the wind from the west); and where he was standing (in front of the Rexall).

Vinny mounted the swordfish on the back wall, where it's been ever since. Except for when some high school kids snuck it out, put it in Ellis Hodge's farm pond and hid in the bushes to watch what would happen. A little while later Ellis drove past and saw a big fin sticking out of the water and rolled to a stop.

Its blue body broke the surface. Why, that's a swordfish, Ellis thought. That's an honest-to-goodness swordfish. Who'd believe it?

A witness—he needed a witness.

He turned his truck around and drove back to the house to get his wife, Miriam. He called Bob Jr. at the *Herald* to come take a picture and grabbed his Zebco 303 rod and reel from the mudroom wall.

By the time Ellis, Miriam, and Bob Jr. converged on the pond, the boys had hauled the swordfish out of the water and were halfway back to town. The boys never told anyone, but for the next three years, always on May 3, they would sneak that fish out of the Coffee Cup and put it in Ellis's pond. Each time Ellis would run to get Miriam and call Bob Jr., who would rush to the pond to no avail.

The boys eventually graduated and left Harmony, but not before giving Ellis a purpose in life. Whenever he drove past that pond he would slow to a crawl. Sometimes he'd take a flashlight and go out there at two in the morning, on the off chance it was a nocturnal swordfish. Ellis referred to it as the Loch Ness of Harmony and devised a theory about how the swordfish ended up in his farm pond.

"It has to do with El Niño. It started out in the Gulf of Mexico and went up the Mississippi River to the Ohio River, then to the Wabash, then to the White River to White Lick Creek, then up that little branch right into my pond. I think it happened during those heavy rains a few years back, when we had that flooding. They say El Niño caused things like this. I've read about it in the paper."

Then Miriam went to visit her sister in the next county. Ellis usually accompanied her, but not this time. It was the third of May. Swordfish Day. This time he'd be ready. He had a net—a big one—and his Zebco 303 rod and reel with a fifty-pound line, and a video camera. He waited all morning. There was a nice bass in the pond; every few minutes it would rise up and break the surface. But Ellis let him be. He was after bigger game.

Noon came. Ellis was hungry. Miriam was gone, and she did all the cooking. She enjoyed it. Every now and then Ellis wanted to go to the Coffee Cup for lunch, but she wouldn't hear of it.

She'd say, "What would people think, seeing you at the Coffee Cup? They'd think we were fighting. No sir, you'll eat right here at home."

So Ellis had never been to the Coffee Cup, but with Miriam gone, today would be the day. He retrieved the video camera and tripod from his truck, inserted a ninety-minute tape, and looked through the viewfinder to be sure it covered the whole pond. Then Ellis jumped in the truck and drove the mile into town to the Coffee Cup. Miriam would never know.

*I*t was almost full. There was one booth open, near the back, next to the liar's table. Penny was right there, handing him a menu and smiling, a coffeepot in her hand. She took his order and stepped aside...and there was the swordfish.

I've seen that fish before, Ellis thought. Then he remembered where. Suddenly he felt self-conscious, like his pants were unzipped or there was toilet paper stuck to his shoe, and he looked around to see if anyone was watching him. But no one was. They were busy eating their beef manhattans and talking about people who weren't there to defend themselves.

Well, to be made a fool of for four years was not a very good feeling. Ellis wondered who had done it. He wondered if they were in the Coffee Cup right now, cackling under their breath. Then if he got up to leave, they'd burst out laughing. So Ellis just sat there and ate his beef manhattan and acted like he belonged.

Vinny came over and sat in the booth across from Ellis. He said, "Hey, Ellis. What did you do to get Miriam so mad?"

Ellis said, "Nothing like that. She's gone to see her sister."

"That's nice," Vinny said. "It's a good thing for families to stay in touch." Vinny said it quietly. He looked sad. He said, "I haven't seen my family since 1963."

Ellis couldn't imagine that. Not seeing your family? He didn't ask why. It wasn't his business.

Instead, he asked, "Where'd you get the swordfish?"

Vinny chuckled. "I caught that on my sixteenth birthday. My old man ran a bait shop and loved to fish, and on my sixteenth birthday he took me deep-sea fishing. I caught that fish and he had it stuffed for me.

"My boy has the most fun with that old thing," Vinny continued. "He put it in White Lick Creek last year and someone thought it was alive and called the police. Can you believe anyone could be that dumb?"

Ellis took another bite of his beef manhattan.

Vinny pulled his wallet from his pocket and plucked out a yellowed picture. It showed a younger Vinny with his father, the swordfish hanging upside down between them.

He said, "My old man wanted me to take over his bait shop. When I told him I didn't want to, he got mad and stopped speaking to me. That's when Penny and I moved here. Haven't seen him since."

It was the first time Vinny had ever told anyone. Ever since he and

Penny had moved here, people had been speculating about their past. Dale Hinshaw, in particular, was all the time hinting that if Vinny had anything to get off his chest, now would be the time to do it. Dale told him how confession was good for the soul, that the Lord loved him and would forgive him. For once, Dale had his theology right.

Vinny looked down at the picture. His father wasn't all bad, Vinny reminisced aloud. He'd taught him how to ride a bicycle and how to make ice cream. Vinny remembered the feel of his father's hand wrapping around his as they turned the crank. He missed his father. The year before, Penny had sent his father a Christmas card. She said it was foolish, these two stubborn men not talking all these years. She forged Vinny's name on it: *Love, Vinny.* And then underneath it she wrote *Your Son* just in case his father had forgotten. Then she mailed it away.

"I don't know, maybe I ought to call him," Vinny said.

"Might not be a bad idea," Ellis said.

*T*hen Ellis said he had to be moving along, that he had work to do, and paid his bill and left. He drove back to the pond, turned off his video recorder, and stowed it in the mudroom closet just as Miriam pulled up in the driveway.

He asked about her sister. She asked if he would like a little something to eat. He told her thanks, but he was fine. He didn't tell her about the swordfish. Driving home from the Coffee Cup, he'd decided never to talk about the swordfish again. He was going to let the matter drop. Maybe people would forget about it after a while.

That Saturday he and Miriam drove to town to do their shopping. They walked past the Coffee Cup. It was closed, the door locked. Dale Hinshaw was standing with his face pressed to the window, peering in. There was a note on the door:

Closed for two weeks.
Will return on the 23rd.
Gone to be with family.

"Looks like that Mafia finally caught up with him," Dale said. "Poor guy."

Ellis said, "You just never know."

And that is true. We just never know. We think we do. We think we have life figured out, and in our arrogance we become hard. But life has a way of humbling us, of softening us. That's what Ellis was thinking as he walked down the sidewalk, holding Miriam's hand—that we don't know the first thing about anything. We're so easily deceived.

When we're young, we think we know all there is to know. Then we grow older, and the more we learn, the more we realize how little we actually know.

It takes a wise man to realize just how much he doesn't know.

five

Revival

*E*very June we hold a revival at Harmony Friends Meeting. These revivals began when I was a kid, which, then, I enjoyed. I especially enjoyed the time Cowboy Bob, the Wild West Evangelist, preached and did rope tricks and told how the devil had him hog-tied, but then Jesus lassoed him and now he wears the kingdom brand. Then he passed out prayer bandannas and invited us to pray the Cowpoke's Prayer: "Dear Lord, I've been a low-down, rotten cowpoke. Take away my black hat and mark me with your kingdom brand. Amen."

Afterwards, Cowboy Bob and his wife, Charlene, sat at the back of the meetinghouse and sold white cowboy hats and musical tapes of Cowboy Bob and the Kingdom Korral singing their favorite gospel tunes of the Old West.

When I was a child I loved listening to Cowboy Bob and all the other evangelists who would visit our church each June. There was Brother Bruno, who found the Lord in prison and became an evangelist. Then came Mohammed the Baptist, who had grown up Muslim and was converted by a missionary. He wore a turban and robes and took kids on camel rides in the parking lot.

When I was in the seventh grade, Miss Marcella Montero came to speak. She had been a 4-H Fair beauty queen, then moved to Hollywood and compromised her morals. Ten years later, she couldn't talk about it without weeping. Thankfully, she had turned from sin, renewed her faith, and taken to the revival circuit where she hinted of past depravities. We waited breathlessly for details, though she was not as forthcoming as we'd have liked.

I loved all this as a child, but now that I'm the pastor, it's a little hard to take. The evangelists come and do rope tricks and tell dramatic stories about their lives of sin before they met the Lord. Sin creative in its originality. Sin we didn't know existed. It is thrilling to listen to, and a little shocking. Then they leave and the next week I step back in the pulpit, and the air is thick with disappointment. It makes me wish I had sinned a bit more before I became a Christian, so I could offer a more colorful testimony.

Truthfully, I was somewhat embarrassed by these evangelists and wanted to dispense with the revivals altogether. So at the April meeting of elders, when Dale Hinshaw brought up the subject of the June revival, I suggested that this might be the year to skip the revival and have a week of prayer instead.

"That's so boring," Fern Hampton said. "Let's think of something else."

It was then that Dale Hinshaw told about Billy Bundle, the World's Shortest Evangelist, who was preaching in the city. Dale had gone to hear him and was greatly impressed by this little man who was so short he couldn't see over the pulpit. He told how Billy took the big pulpit Bible, placed it on the floor, said "Thy Word is a lamp unto my feet," then stepped up on that Bible to preach.

Dale Hinshaw was captivated and vowed to bring the World's Shortest Evangelist to Harmony Friends Meeting as our June revival speaker.

"You should have seen the crowd," Dale exclaimed. "The place was packed. The offering was so big they had to empty the baskets halfway through. We do this right and we can maybe raise enough money to buy new cabinets for the church kitchen."

Fern Hampton said, "I'm for that."

So that is how Billy Bundle, the World's Shortest Evangelist, came to speak at the June revival of Harmony Friends Meeting.

*B*illy Bundle hadn't always been an evangelist. He'd started out as a professional wrestler. My brother Roger and I used to watch him Saturday afternoons on Channel 5. The wrestling matches were held at the armory in the city. If we wrapped tin foil around the television antennas and slid it up and down, Channel 5 would come in clear. We were little kids, and professional wrestling made a great impression. We'd push the furniture back to the walls and wrestle in our underwear, just like Billy Bundle.

Except that they didn't call him Billy Bundle on television. They called him "The Mississippi Midget," even though he wasn't from Mississippi, nor was he a midget. He was from the Bronx and came from a long line of short people. He spoke in a Southern drawl and wore bright red wrestling trunks. As he walked to and from the ring, he wore a top hat, which he took off in the presence of ladies. A Southern gentleman.

Billy was one of the good guys, at least at first. Then he became one of the bad guys and would kick his opponent when the referee wasn't watching. He hid brass knuckles in his trunks, which the referees never found. He hit below the belt. He was an easy man to hate.

Then Billy had his accident, which everyone watching Channel 5 witnessed. He got tangled in the ropes and fell and broke his right leg, which caused him to limp for the rest of his life.

While Billy was in the hospital he watched Channel 21, the religion station, and realized his true calling: evangelism. He quit the wrestling business and began traveling from town to town, preaching revivals. On the last night of the revivals, Billy would do a dramatization from the book of Genesis, Jacob wrestling with the stranger at the river Jabbok. He would ask for a volunteer from the audience, who he would fling around the platform, using flips and body slams and headlocks. At the stirring conclusion of his story, you'd hear a loud *c-r-a-c-k* and Billy would rise to his feet, grimacing, and hobble away—just like Jacob. It always brought in a good offering, and afterwards Billy would autograph pictures of himself dressed in his wrestling trunks, back when he was "The Mississippi Midget."

This was the man Dale Hinshaw chose to bring a message from the eternal God.

The revival lasted three nights—Thursday, Friday, and Saturday. The weekend before, the Friendly Women's Circle posted fliers at the Laundromat, the Krogers, and in the front window of the Coffee Cup. Bob Miles Jr. ran an article in the *Herald* about Billy, chronicling his early years in the Bronx, his fame as a championship wrestler, and his triumph as the World's Shortest Evangelist. He printed a picture of Billy in his red wrestling trunks, holding a Bible. Bob didn't even put it in the religion section, where no one would notice. He slapped it right on the front page, up in the left corner next to the weather, where everyone looked.

On Thursday afternoon I went to the Coffee Cup and Billy Bundle was all they were talking about. They remembered watching him on Channel 5.

"For a little fella, he was some wrestler," Bob Miles Sr. was saying. "He'd grab hold of someone at the knees and they couldn't shake him loose. He'd hang on tight and wear 'em down. He was a real American, too. He'd spit out his gum before the national anthem. Not like these athletes nowadays."

*B*illy drove into town later that day in his van with *The World's Shortest Evangelist* painted on the side. I could see his head just above the steering wheel. He bounded from the van and shook my hand. He squeezed it hard, as if handshaking were less a greeting and more a contest.

I took him inside the meetinghouse, showed him the pulpit, and asked what he would be speaking on.

"The Lord told me to preach on spiritual warfare," Billy said. "You're gonna love it. On the last night, I wear military fatigues—special made—and I march into the church to "The Stars and Stripes Forever." It's a sight to see. People snap to when they see me come in. They know I mean business."

I asked, "Does this mean you're not going to dress like Jacob and wrestle with the stranger at the river Jabbok?"

"No, that was last year's gig," he said. "This year I'm a soldier."

He stayed at our house, a minor detail Dale Hinshaw had forgotten to mention. I told Dale we didn't have an extra bed.

"That's okay, Sam," Dale said. "Billy can have your bedroom. It's only for three days. Our Lord slept in a tomb that long. Surely you can give up your bed."

So Billy slept in our bed while Barbara and I slept on the pullout couch in the living room, the metal bar gouging our backs. We could hear Billy's snoring through the heat ducts.

I was raised to believe I could do anything I put my mind to. I put my mind to liking Billy Bundle, but failed.

On his first night of preaching, Billy revealed how liberalism had invaded the church through pastors who'd studied left-wing theology at fancy schools in the city. He looked at me as he spoke. He told how, when the Lord returned, there'd be some pastors getting set straight.

"Amen," Dale Hinshaw shouted.

On Friday night, Billy brought to light a secret code he had discovered in the Old Testament book of Obadiah. Bible scholars had studied Obadiah for thousands of years, but God had seen fit to reveal this secret to Billy Bundle, the World's Shortest Evangelist.

"I know *when* the Lord will return," shouted Billy. "The very date. I know *where* it'll happen. I know *how* it'll happen."

"Bring it on," Dale Hinshaw yelled.

On Saturday night the meetinghouse was full. Word had gotten out that Billy had something special in store. He wore his soldier's outfit and marched in to "The Stars and Stripes Forever."

Dale Hinshaw leapt to his feet and saluted.

At the end of his message, Billy gave an altar call. He invited anyone who wanted to enlist in Billy's Army to come forward for recruitment. Six people came forward, the same six who always go forward. If I had been their general, I'd have gone AWOL.

Billy left early Sunday morning, to my deep relief. I waved good-bye to him from the curb in front of our house. I watched as his van turned the corner and headed down Main Street toward the city. I prayed he would never return.

When I preached that morning I spoke of how, when Jesus walked this earth, He warned of false prophets, of ravenous wolves draped in sheep's wool. How He told His followers the false prophets would bear bad fruit, so watch them close. Do not judge, He told His followers, but be wise. Be fruit inspectors.

"You will know them by their fruits," Jesus taught.

Then I sat in the Quaker silence thinking of Billy's fruit—self-gratification before God's glory, ignorance above wisdom, trickery over truth.

As he prepared to leave earlier that morning, Billy had told me he was booked through the year.

"The calls are rolling in," he confided. "I'm thinking of upping my fee."

That Tuesday, three people came to prayer meeting. I wondered why it was that only three people cared to gather to talk with God, while the World's Shortest Evangelist could pack a church full.

I tried not to be discouraged. But I had an inkling how Jesus must have felt when all the folks fled Him at the end, chasing off to find someone a bit more fun to follow.

I know one thing for sure: Cowboy Bob, the Wild West Evangelist, was right all along. Sometimes we're just low-down, rotten cowpokes, needing to be marked with the kingdom brand.

Six
Uly

*M*y best friend in childhood was Uly Grant. At school we sat in alphabetical order, so Uly sat just behind me in Fern Hampton's first-grade classroom.

I had known Uly before that because his family owned Harmony's hardware store, the Grant Hardware Emporium. It was a big brick building with a display window full of Zebco fishing rods, Schwinn bicycles, and Case pocketknives. I would stand and look at them on Saturday mornings. There was a Miss Hardware calendar back in the corner office, which I wasn't permitted to stand and look at.

Uly Grant was alleged to be a direct descendant of Ulysses S. Grant, the Civil War general and United States president. The town folklore was that the general's son, Ulysses S. Grant II, began the Grant Hardware Emporium in 1876. Like his father, the younger Grant yearned for life on the battlefield. But then he fell in love with a Quaker from our town—a Miss Penelope Hastings. She was unusually beautiful, and he was so stricken with love that he went to her father and asked for her hand in marriage.

"She's not mine to give away," her father said. "Ask her yourself."

So he did, and Penelope declined his proposal. She told him, "I cannot in good conscience marry a man whose business is the destruction of human life."

Those old Quakers were not to be trifled with.

Ulysses S. Grant II tried to forget Penelope, but couldn't. Her beauty was etched on his mind. In 1870, he surrendered his military commission and they were married at the Harmony Friends meetinghouse. President Grant was not present, in deep opposition to his son marrying a Quaker and fathering pacifist children.

They stayed in Harmony, where U.S. Grant II became a Quaker and founded the Grant Hardware Emporium in 1872. He built it on the southwest corner of the town square, where it still sits—one block west of the Harmony Public Library and next to the Johnny Mackey Funeral Home.

In the early years of their marriage, accounts of President Grant's drunken behavior reached Harmony, though the subject was never raised in his son's presence. His son was grieved and pledged never to imbibe. Even as I was growing up, we avoided the topic. When we studied the U.S. presidents in sixth grade and came to Ulysses S. Grant, Miss Fishbeck gave a nervous smile, glanced at Uly, and said, "Ulysses S. Grant was our eighteenth president. He was a great general and a fine man, except for one weakness which need not be mentioned."

Then she moved quickly to Rutherford B. Hayes, who never drank anything except water and lemonade.

*I*t was the custom in Harmony for Mr. Squier, the history teacher, to take the eighth graders on a bus trip the week after school let out. We'd work all through the year raising money—selling popcorn at the basketball games, holding car washes, and selling Christmas fruitcakes door to door. People would see us coming and bolt their doors.

I remember the year it was our turn to go. The first Monday of summer vacation, Uly and I stood, bleary eyed, on the sidewalk in front of the junior high school at five in the morning. We waited in the damp air with the other kids and Mr. Squier and a few adult chaperones, waiting for the charter bus from the city to roll down Main Street, past Harvey Muldock's car dealership, and up the park hill before pulling to the curb in front of the school.

It was a blue diesel bus with reclining seats and headrests and a bathroom at the back, which was in constant use the entire trip. It was pure fascination—a bathroom on a bus. We wondered what happened when you flushed the toilet. Uly thought maybe everything just sort of fell down on the road. We weren't sure. We asked Mr. Squier where it went.

He said, "There's a holding tank at the back of the bus. It goes there. The only thing is, if the bus gets hit from behind, that tank will explode, and if that happens, you want to be sure to duck."

Uly and I moved up front behind the driver and put on our raincoats.

*U*ly was lucky to be going. For the past twenty-three years the eighth graders had gone to Washington, D.C., but Mr. Squier was tiring of that city. Twenty-three years in a row had tested his enthusiasm. He was looking for something new, something fresh, which was when he hatched the idea of our class touring the Civil War battle sites of the South.

We'd start with Antietam and move on to Shiloh, then Chancellorsville and Chickamauga. We'd point the bus toward Charleston, South Carolina, where the Great Sorrow had begun on April 12 in the year of our Lord 1861. On the way home, we'd stop at the Appomattox Court House where the war had limped to its tired end.

Mr. Squier sent home a note to our parents announcing the trip.

That's when Uly's father, Ulysses S. Grant IV, said Uly couldn't go.

He told Uly, "Us Grants aren't welcome in those parts. It's not safe. They'd make you disappear. There's people down there; they still remember it. They're bitter. You'd end up in some jail and never see the light of day. That ain't Mayberry down there, son. Not for us Grants. You're staying home."

This troubled Mr. Squier. Uly had sold more fruitcakes than anyone, so this just wasn't fair. Mr. Squier went to Uly's house to talk with his father. He brought a brand-new wallet with him. He sat at their kitchen table and opened the wallet to the plastic picture holders and pulled out the paper I.D. card and began to write. Except he didn't write Uly's real name. He made up a name, *Bob Lee,* and showed it to Mr. Grant. Uly's father studied it a moment and asked, "You think it'll work?"

"I think so," said Mr. Squier. And that's how we smuggled Ulysses S. Grant V, alias Bob Lee, into Chickamauga, Georgia.

I didn't see much of Uly after high school. I went on to college and Uly stayed behind to take over the Grant Hardware Emporium from his father. The Emporium was in shambles. Uly's father had forgotten the Lord and the Emporium and, despite the pleas of his sainted mother, had taken up drink.

I remember, as a child, watching Uly's daddy lifting a bottle from his desk drawer and taking a long pull. I remember Uly staring in fascination. I remember smelling alcohol on Uly's breath in high school, our senior year. I thought it was a youthful urge which would fade with time, but for Uly it only grew stronger.

In college, when I would come home for Christmas, my mother would tell me about seeing Uly wobble out of the Buckhorn Tavern. But now Uly didn't even bother with the Buckhorn. The conversation there distracted him from his main purpose, which was to get drunk.

Which is what he did every night in his basement, with his little boys looking on.

Uly would close the Hardware Emporium at five P.M., walk the four blocks home, and sit in his basement and drink. His three sons would sit on the basement steps and watch him, fascinated, just as Uly had watched his own father years before.

I suspect Uly's three sons were the reason he finally called me after I moved home to Harmony. It was two o'clock in the morning when the phone rang. Uly asked if I could come over to his basement. I dressed, walked down the alleyway to his house the next block over, let myself in the back door, and eased down the basement stairs. It was dark. Uly was sitting in the corner, a bottle in his hand.

"Have a drink," he said, and offered me the bottle.

"No thanks, Uly, I don't drink," I said.

He started talking. "Sam, remember that trip we took in the eighth grade? Remember that bus with the toilet? Wasn't that some trip?"

He kept on talking, then he fell asleep. I went back up the stairs, down the alley, and back to bed. I lay in bed, staring at the ceiling, thinking of Uly.

Next afternoon I went to the Hardware Emporium to talk with him. Uly was sitting in the corner office underneath the Miss Hardware calendar. He looked up and smiled and said, "Hey, Sam, long time no see. How ya been?"

He called again a month later, late at night, inviting me over to talk about old times. I told him no. Told him we'd talk the next day, that I'd stop by to see him at the Emporium.

The next morning, I sat on the bench in front of the Emporium waiting for Uly. His wife and boys came at eight o'clock to open up. I asked her where Uly was.

"Sleeping it off," she said. "I'm not sure how much more of this I can take."

I walked over to Uly's house and let myself in. He was asleep down in the basement, on the floor next to the washer. I helped him up the stairs and sat him at the kitchen table.

I took a chair across the table from him. He raised his head and moaned. I looked him straight in his bloodshot eyes and said, "Uly, you are a drunk. If you don't get help soon, you're going to lose your family. Is that what you want?"

He began to cry. No, it wasn't what he wanted, he told me. He'd been trying to stop. Trying so hard, so long.

Uly was still a member of Harmony Friends Meeting, though he came only on Easter and at Christmas. He had been inoculated with a small dose of Christianity, which had kept him from catching the real thing.

I talked about Uly at the next elders' meeting. I said we needed to pray for him, and that we needed to start an Alcoholics Anonymous chapter at our meeting.

"How much will that cost?" Dale Hinshaw asked.

Dale liked a bargain. He was all for helping people as long as it didn't cost anything. Every year when we had a revival, he would take the cost of the evangelist, divide it by souls saved, and announce the results in church the next Sunday. The week after Billy Bundle, the World's Shortest Evangelist, Dale stood and announced that we had saved six souls at a cost of eighty-six dollars per soul. "Time was," Dale concluded, "when you could save a soul for under ten dollars." He longed for those days.

I told Dale an AA chapter wouldn't cost anything. That all we had to do was provide a place for them to meet and set out cookies.

His eyes lit up. "The alcoholics would come here? To our church?"

"Yes," Miriam Hodge said, "but we don't want you showing up the nights they meet to see who has a drinking problem. Is that understood?"

Miriam talked about how her uncle had had a drinking problem, and how she wished there had been someone to help him.

I asked how folks could find out about the program.

Dale Hinshaw suggested sending a flier to everyone in town we thought was a drunk. He started making a list with Uly's name at the top.

Miriam said, "Put that list away. You can't do it that way. We'll contact the AA people and they'll help us get it going."

Which we did. We looked them up in the city phone book, and they sent a man to talk with us about starting a Harmony chapter of Alcoholics Anonymous. We would need a leader. But the leader had to be an alcoholic, and no one in Harmony would admit to meeting that criterion, so we had to import an alcoholic from the city.

*H*is name was Gary. That was the first thing he told us when he came to the following month's elders' meeting.

"My name is Gary, and I'm an alcoholic," he said. Then he told us his story. Dale sat listening, enthralled, as Gary recalled his years of hard living and how he'd found a new life in a church basement in Ohio.

When Gary finished speaking, Dale leaned back in his chair and marveled, "Well, imagine that; and it was free!"

Gary said he'd need an assistant, someone to work alongside him, someone who could take over after he was gone. I told him about Uly. Gary said, "Let's go see him right now."

Gary was not your typical AA member. He wasn't the type to sit around in a church basement waiting for drunks to come to him. He was a Green Beret type of AA member who believed in active intervention.

We walked over to Uly's house. Uly was in his basement, just getting started. Gary reached out with one hand and lifted Uly to his feet, and with the other hand took that bottle and poured it down the utility sink next to the washing machine.

He stared at Uly. He said, "You are pathetic. Sitting down here in your basement drinking your life away in front of your boys. What kind of man are you?"

Uly hung his head.

Gary growled, "Look at me when I'm talking to you."

Uly raised up.

Gary said, "I'm going to help you, then you're going to help me help others. You're going to be my assistant. Have I made myself clear? As of this moment, you will no longer drink. I want you to say that, Uly. I want you to say, 'I am Ulysses S. Grant the Fifth, and I no longer drink.' Say it."

Uly whimpered, "I am Ulysses S. Grant the Fifth, and I no longer drink."

Gary said, "I can't hear you."

Uly said it even louder. "I am Ulysses S. Grant the Fifth, and I no longer drink."

I'm not certain what it was. I think it was heritage rising up. Whatever it was, something was born in Uly that evening; something old and deep within him rose up and took hold of him and made him new.

He rose to his feet and moved forward to Appomattox, to victory. He marched up the basement stairs, up from that dungeon of death, and didn't look back.

The alcoholics met every Wednesday at seven P.M. in the church basement. Dale Hinshaw would arrive at six-thirty and set out the cookies, then leave before anyone got there.

Gary and Uly would arrive at a quarter till and go over their battle plans.

"This is war," Gary would remind him. "We're fighting for people's lives. Don't you ever forget that."

Uly started coming to church. Every Sunday. Brought his wife and his boys and sat on the sixth row, in Fern Hampton's pew. For sixty-five years, that pew had not been sat in by anyone outside the Hampton family. As her mother lay dying, Fern pledged she would guard that pew with her life. But on that day, Fern looked up at Uly and his family and smiled and slid right over. There are those who claim that was a bigger miracle than Uly Grant's sobriety.

Dale Hinshaw was beside himself. He stood during the silence and said, "One saved soul, and all it cost was cookies. What a bargain!"

After church, Uly proceeded directly to the Emporium, took down the Miss Hardware calendar and threw it in the trash.

"It's the straight path from here on out," he told his wife.

Then one Wednesday, Gary phoned Uly at the Hardware Emporium.

"I won't be there tonight," he told Uly. "I'm needed elsewhere. I'm leaving you in command. I need you to take the hill. Can you do it?"

Uly rose to his feet and shouted into the phone, "Yes, sir. I can do it, sir!"

And Uly did it. He marched down to the church basement and at seven o'clock rose to his feet and declared, "My name is Uly, and I'm an alcoholic."

Thus are the changes wrought in a man's life—that courage is treasured more than comfort and, in that choice, victory is gained.

Summer

Seven

Miss Rudy, Wilbur, and Friday Nights

I've always loved books, ever since I was in the first grade and my mother promised if I read a book a week, she would give me a dime for an ice cream cone at the Dairy Queen.

We lived one mile from the library. On Saturday mornings she would tuck a dime in my pocket, walk me to the front door, and point me toward the library.

"It's that way," she'd tell me, pointing east. "A big, brick building. You can't miss it."

I'd walk east on Mill Street to Cook Avenue, down Cook Avenue to Marian Street, then past the Grant Hardware Emporium to the Harmony Public Library. The library was built in 1903 with a donation from Andrew Carnegie, who had made a fortune in steel and had given money for thousands of libraries.

I'd walk through the front door. There would be Miss Rudy, perched on a stool behind the counter. I'd turn in my book, almost always a biography. I love biographies. To this day, my head is filled with little known facts about obscure historical figures: DeWitt Clinton, builder of the Erie Canal; Bernard Baruch, businessman and statesman;

and William Almon Wheeler, United States vice president from 1877 to 1881. When he died, though, no one noticed he was dead until 1882. He was a very private man. Plus, in 1881 we had three presidents and in all the excitement no one noticed the death of Vice President William Almon Wheeler.

He was appointed vice president by Rutherford B. Hayes, who left office in early 1881 and forgot to take William Almon Wheeler with him. Then James Garfield became president. Unfortunately, Garfield was assassinated before appointing a new vice president. No one told William Almon Wheeler to leave, so he just sort of hung around. When Garfield was killed, William Almon Wheeler was ready to assume the presidency, but Chester Arthur said, "I'm in charge here" and took over. He was pushy that way.

Before William Almon Wheeler became vice president, he was a librarian. He only became vice president because it allowed him more time to read, and it paid better. He was Rutherford B. Hayes's college roommate and had never earned much money, so when Rutherford B. Hayes offered him the vice presidency, Wheeler jumped at it. Then, while attending a state dinner, he met Andrew Carnegie, the philanthropist. They were seated at the same table, and Andrew Carnegie was pondering what to do with his money. He couldn't decide whether to buy a baseball team or give money to build libraries.

William Almon Wheeler leaned over and whispered in his ear, "Baseball is a fad. If you give your money for libraries, your name will be famous in every city and hamlet throughout the land. It will be your legacy."

So that's what Andrew Carnegie did. Today, everyone knows who Andrew Carnegie is because of the Carnegie libraries, while William Almon Wheeler, despite being a man of vision, rests in obscurity. No one knows anything about him unless he's read his biography, which I did when I was in the third grade.

But not many people have read it. I was at the Harmony Public Library the first week of summer and came across *William Almon Wheeler: Man of Vision,* opened it and looked on the due-date card to see who else had checked it out. My name was the last on the card. *Sam Gardner.* It had been carefully printed by Miss Rudy, along with the return date, *May 3, 1970.* There was a Coke ring on the cover from where my brother had used the book as a coaster, which Miss Rudy lectured me about when I returned the book.

I remember handing it to her. Remember her looking at it, then peering over her glasses at me and saying, "You need to take care of these books. You wouldn't set a Coke on your Bible, would you? You take better care of these books, or we won't let you check them out."

I was terrified. No more books. That would be tragic. I loved books. I loved going to the library on Saturday mornings when the other boys were playing basketball in the school gymnasium. Loved walking up and down the rows of books and tilting my head and reading the titles. Loved looking through the biographies, especially the *Childhood of Famous Americans* series. Then walking over to the adult fiction shelves and pulling out the due-date cards to see who had read certain books. That was always enlightening.

People who I thought were pillars of the community and saints of the church had read certain books Pastor Taylor had cautioned us about. Books like *Gone with the Wind,* which had a bad word in it, a word we Christians didn't use, even though Miss Rudy had scratched out the bad word and written the word *hoot* above it. So that Rhett Butler said to Scarlett O'Hara, "Frankly, my dear, I don't give a hoot."

If you went to the circulation desk to ask if the library had a certain book and Miss Rudy didn't think it was one suitable for Christian people, she would let you know.

She'd say, "We don't have that book. This is a library, not a cesspool. If you want smut, you'll have to go to the city."

She'd say it in a loud voice, so that people would look up from whatever they were reading and stare at you. By the time you reached home, three people had phoned your mother to tell on you.

*M*iss Rudy attended the Quaker meeting, though it pained her to do so. The elders would stand at the pulpit and read the Scripture and would mispronounce the words, and she would wince. They would read about the ten *leapers* whom Jesus healed, and she would flinch as if someone had struck her with a whip.

The worst Sunday of all was when Pastor Taylor called on Wilbur Matthews to come forward and read a passage of Scripture. It took Wilbur five minutes to read three verses, and one of them was "Jesus wept." Five painful minutes, and even then he couldn't do it. Finally Wilbur said he couldn't see without his glasses and sat down, to everyone's relief. No one suspected anything, except for Miss Rudy, who thought, *Wilbur Matthews can't read.* And poor Wilbur was so embarrassed, so ashamed, he stopped coming to church.

Miss Rudy went to visit him. She knocked on his front door. Wilbur opened the door. She said, "We've missed you at church, Wilbur."

He said, "Well, I've been awful busy. I've had lots to do. You know how it is."

Miss Rudy said, "Wilbur, I can teach you how to read."

Wilbur blustered, "What do you mean? I know how to read."

Miss Rudy stared him down. "Wilbur," she said, "I know when a man can't read."

Wilbur began weeping. He was ashamed. He could scarcely read. All these years he'd kept it a secret. But now he was tired of the deception, of patting his pockets like he was searching for glasses. A man can keep a secret only so long. He blurted out, "I can't read and I'm too old to learn. I'm a dumb, old man."

Miss Rudy said, "Don't talk that way. You come to the library this Friday at closing time and we'll start."

So Wilbur went.

I would walk past the library with my brother Roger on the way to the Dairy Queen after supper on Friday nights. We would drop our books in the outside depository and we'd see the lights on. The doors would be locked. We'd press our faces to the glass and watch Miss Rudy hold up flashcards and watch Wilbur Matthews frown and study each card and then blurt something out.

If he got it right, Miss Rudy would smile. If he wasn't right, we could read her lips: "Try again, Wilbur." And he'd try again and keep trying, until he got it right.

He went to the library every Friday night for one year. Miss Rudy never told anyone and neither did he. Sometimes I would see him over at the biographies, looking through the *Childhood of Famous Americans* series.

After several months, Wilbur came back to church, and when the pastor asked for a volunteer to read the Scripture, Wilbur raised his hand and eased out of his pew and walked down front to the pulpit. That long walk down. All those people watching. All those people thinking, Oh no, not Wilbur.

Wilbur was scared. His hands shook as he opened his Bible. Then he glanced down and there was Miss Rudy on the third row, right side, and she smiled at him and mouthed the words, "You can do it." And he did. He read about the ten lepers whom Jesus had healed and how only one had the decency to thank Him. When Wilbur finished reading, he closed his Bible and looked down to the third row at Miss Rudy and said, "Thank you, Miss Rudy."

She mouthed the words, "You're welcome, Wilbur. You're welcome."

No one knew what he meant, except for my brother and me—and we never told. Oh, people talked about it. They speculated about it on account of Miss Rudy wasn't married. Why did Wilbur thank her? What did she do? What was going on? But Roger and I never told, and Wilbur and Miss Rudy never told either. Then people forgot about it, until one year later when Wilbur Matthews died and left his money to the library, and no one knew why, except for Roger and me and we weren't talking. The library added on a room and Miss Rudy hired the town jeweler to make a brass plaque that read

In Memory of
Wilbur Matthews—
A Man of Courage

This summer they built on to the library, and the Wilbur Matthews Room is gone. I was there when a worker pried off the brass plaque and it bent, and he turned to his boss and asked, "Do you suppose we oughtta keep this?"

His boss said, "Naw, you can pitch it." And that's what he did. I watched him do it. He pitched it in a wastebasket.

But I retrieved that plaque, took it home and straightened it out and polished it. I'm going to go back to the library, sneak over to the biography section, to the *Childhood of Famous Americans* series, and find the book titled *William Almon Wheeler: Man of Vision*. I'm going to put Wilbur's plaque in that book. It'll be safe there. No one ever reads it. If someone does find it, years from now, it'll be a mystery. They'll look at that plaque and wonder who Wilbur Matthews was and why he was a man of courage. But I won't tell. It's a secret and I intend to keep it that way.

I've lived in Harmony 'most all my life, in this same little town. I walk up and down the same streets I did years ago, past the same houses and same people sitting on their porches. But underneath the visible lies the invisible—our shameful secrets, our quiet shames.

Then we get found out and brace ourselves for ridicule, but are visited with grace. Grace knocks on our door and pays us a visit. Just like Miss Rudy. Grace takes us by the hand and says, "That's not so bad. I've heard worse. Let's see if we can make things better."

When love takes you by the hand and leaves you better, that is home. That's the place to stake your claim and build your life. You might never get written about in the *Childhood of Famous Americans* series, but there are deeper blessings to be had.

Eight

Burma-Shave

G rowing up after church on Sundays, we would eat Sunday dinner at my grandparents' house. At precisely twelve-thirty the grandfather clock in the downstairs hallway would dong, which signaled that dinner was on the table. The children would come in from the front yard and the men would rise up from the rockers on the porch and we would make our way in to the feast.

Except on the last Sunday of the month, which was when we had to stay after church for the monthly business meeting. On that day, we ate cold meat loaf sandwiches left over from my grandmother's Saturday night meat loaf. The cold meat loaf sandwiches were the highlight of the day. I'd put ketchup on mine and squish the bread flat around the meat, then dip it in ketchup again to ease the dryness.

The business meetings were long and tedious, chock-full of detailed reports on trifling matters. The meeting would begin with a devotional thought from Bob Miles Sr., former editor of *The Harmony Herald* and teacher of the Live Free or Die Sunday school class. Bob Sr. would begin by recalling how much of the week he'd spent in earnest prayer, seeking God's counsel on what message he might bring. But it was obvious to us that Bob had forgotten all about the devotional until that very moment and was merely biding his time until a thought worth sharing came to mind. The devotional took fifteen minutes and always ended with Bob cautioning against the United Nations.

After the devotional thought, the meeting clerk would call for the treasurer's report. The head usher, Dale Hinshaw, would bring forward the Florsheim shoebox where he stored the month's offering and would spread the money on a table and count it in front of everyone. Twice. Pastor Taylor often said that if we gave, a good measure would be given to us. Pressed down, shaken together, and running over. But in all the years I've been here, I've never seen Dale's shoebox run over.

The best part of the monthly business meeting was when the elders gave their report. The elders were a fascination to me—upright saints of the church, meeting in the basement on the third Thursday of every month to shepherd us along. They would keep careful notes which they shared with the rest of us, except when it concerned certain scandalous topics that could not be made public. Then they would just say, "We discussed several matters of a confidential nature."

That always intrigued me. I would sit in the fifth pew and speculate about such things. My father was an elder, and I would try to pry information from him to no avail. He would look at me and say, "There's some things you're better off not knowing."

I'd reply, "Why don't you tell me what they are, and let me be the judge of that?" He would fix me with a long stare.

I always wanted to be an elder and learn the church's secrets, so you can imagine my delight when I became the pastor and started attending the elders' meetings down in the basement on the third Thursday of every month.

*T*he delight was short lived. At the June meeting, Dale Hinshaw asked for prayers for his nephew who, after siring five children in six years, had gotten a vasectomy and was in great pain. The doctor told him to keep ice on it, but his wife had forgotten to fill the ice trays so he used a bag of frozen peas instead. His children kept asking why their daddy was walking around with frozen peas in his underwear.

Dale said, "That's not all of it. He doesn't sleep well, on account of he has thin eyelids and the streetlights keep him up. He doesn't get near enough sleep. Three, maybe four hours a night. He's having a time of it."

We promised to pray for him, then quickly moved on to another subject, not wanting to dwell on Dale's nephew with thin eyelids and peas in his pants. Miriam Hodge wrote in the notes, *We discussed a matter of a confidential nature.*

Then we discussed several other matters, none of which had any bearing on the kingdom of God. This is what happens when you have elders who fancy themselves great philosophers. They can wax eloquent about eternal truths as long as it doesn't get personal. Everyone is an expert. Everyone has a firm opinion about what we ought to do and no one gives an inch. If we accidentally appoint a saint to the elder's committee, by midyear we have broken them of all Christlike tendencies.

We nearly ruined Miriam Hodge. We appointed her to serve as the head elder after Dale Hinshaw nominated himself to the committee. We put her in charge to offset the "Dale Hinshaw Effect." The Dale Hinshaw Effect is simply this: If there is a bad idea to be thought, Dale Hinshaw will think it.

Before Miriam took charge, a typical elders' meeting would go like this: At 7:10 P.M. the elders drive up in the meetinghouse parking lot, ten minutes late. The first one to arrive makes the coffee. They stand in the kitchen until the coffee is brewed, then set up a table in the basement and talk about basketball and the state of our country, which according to them is bad and getting worse. This takes one hour. Then they discuss matters of a confidential nature, then go home flush with accomplishment. If someone thinks of it, they close with prayer.

Miriam Hodge arrived fifteen minutes early for our first meeting. She made the coffee. She stood at the door and greeted her fellow elders, and handed them an agenda. The others were mystified. An agenda? What was this? What's going on here? First item: prayer. Miriam worked her way around the table, inviting each elder to identify a spiritual need in his life, then encouraging the rest of us to pray for that person.

All the other elders are men. Men not accustomed to spiritual introspection. There was lots of "Umm, I'll have to give that some thought. I was thinking we were going to talk about painting the meetinghouse."

Paint, they can talk about. It's personal confession that throws them for a loop.

That was when Dale Hinshaw, in a valiant effort to keep the focus off his own spirituality, began talking about his nephew's vasectomy and thin eyelids.

But Miriam held to the agenda and moved to the next item, my vacation. Dale Hinshaw began recalling vacations he'd taken. He told about when he was little and his father would drive them to the lake. He recalled reading the old Burma-Shave shaving cream signs posted along the road. There, that was something they could talk about— Burma-Shave signs. That was safe ground. Asa Peacock and Dale began recalling their favorites:

> *The whale put Jonah down the hatch*
> *but coughed him up because he scratched.*
> *Burma-Shave*
> *The monkey took one look at Jim*
> *and threw the peanuts back at him.*
> *Burma-Shave*

It would be more fun to go by air
but we can't put these signs up there.
Burma-Shave

Dale Hinshaw especially liked this one:

In this world of toil and sin
your head goes bald but not your chin.
Burma-Shave

It took thirty minutes for Miriam to get them back to the next agenda item, church growth. Our numbers were down, and had been for thirty years. Miriam had drawn up a graph tracing our attendance. If it had been snow, we could have sledded down it.

Dale Hinshaw thought maybe it was time to hold another revival. Maybe have two revivals a year. He talked about a church in Florida that had a revival every week. Maybe we could do that. Harvey Muldock suggested putting a lottery ticket in each bulletin. Miriam suggested we become sensitive to the Spirit's leading and begin inviting people to worship with us. They decided to go with the lottery idea.

*N*ext Monday, the phone rang. It was Miriam.

"We've got problems," she said. "I'll be by to pick you up."

I sat on the porch, waiting and worried. Five minutes later, Miriam pulled her truck to the curb in front of my house. We drove west of town, then turned around and headed back toward Harmony.

There they were. Signs. Just like Burma-Shave used to use. The first one was on the edge of town, just before the *Welcome to Harmony* sign:

If you cheat and drink and lie
turn to God before you die.
Harmony Friends Meeting

Miriam asked if I knew who put the signs up. I had my suspicions.
We drove east of town. Turned back. More signs.

The gate is narrow, the path is straight.
Follow Jesus. Don't be late.
Harmony Friends Meeting

"Dale Hinshaw," I told Miriam. "This has Dale Hinshaw written all
over it."

We drove toward the meetinghouse. More signs. This time in front
of Harvey Muldock's car dealership.

Go to church and learn to pray
or when you die there's Hell to pay.
Harmony Friends Meeting

Dale Hinshaw was pounding in the last sign as we pulled up to the
meetinghouse curb. It read, *Tired of sin? Come on in!* Dale smiled and said,
"Catchy, isn't it? I think it'll take care of our church growth problem."

He told how the Lord had spoken to him in a dream. He dreamt he
was a boy again, riding in the backseat toward the lake and reading the
Burma-Shave signs. Then he woke up and went to his kitchen table and
the Lord gave him those gospel messages. Just like that.

He turned to Miriam. "I have you to thank. If you hadn't encouraged us to follow the Spirit's leading, this never would have happened."

Miriam paled. This wasn't what she'd had in mind.

All week long, people called, wanting me to take down the signs. I told them to talk with Dale.

On Thursday morning I walked to the meetinghouse, past the *Tired of sin? Come on in!* sign. Someone had written underneath it, *If not, call 555-9658.* That was my phone number. All week long my phone rang. Apparently, people in this town weren't tired of sin.

*T*hen Sunday came, and the meetinghouse was packed. People who hadn't come for years were washed and starched and sitting with their hands folded in prayer.

They were there for the lottery tickets, but Dale didn't know that. He thought it was the signs. He was deeply pleased. He talked about making more signs, of putting them up all over town. Maybe even go statewide. "We could do our own TV show," he went on, "just like that Robert Schula fella with that church you can see through."

There would be no stopping him now.

It's a dangerous thing to ask the Spirit to lead you. You never know what might happen. But it doesn't mean we should stop asking. Even though we get our wires crossed, we need to keep at it. Because someday someone might grow tired of sin and walk right in. And when they do, we need to be here for them.

> *Turn toward home. We'll be here.*
> *God is gracious. Don't you fear.*

Nine

The Birds and the Bees

The day before Billy Bundle, the World's Shortest Evangelist, came to preach our revival, it occurred to me I needed a secretary. Back in April, the elders had put me in charge of calling Bob Miles Jr. at the *Herald* to arrange publicity, which I forgot to do even though I had written it on my to-do list: *Call B.M. regarding B.B.* I spent the next two months trying to decipher my own note, and by the time I figured it out, Billy Bundle was on his way.

At first I thought I was supposed to call Bea Majors about the Bible Bonanza where we donated Bibles to the Choctaw Indians, but when I called to remind her she said the Bible Bonanza wasn't for another eight months. Then I thought it meant I was supposed to call Bill Muldock about buying new baseball bats for our men's softball team, not that it would help. In fifteen years, our men's softball team had won only one game. We beat the Friendly Women's Circle, who rallied in the last inning when my grandmother hit a home run. We squeaked out a one-run victory, just barely.

It wasn't until Dale Hinshaw phoned to ask why our revival ad wasn't in the *Herald* that I figured out that *Call B.M. regarding B.B.* meant

"Call Bob Miles regarding Billy Bundle." I explained to Dale what had happened, then suggested that if I had a secretary these mistakes could be avoided.

The reason I didn't have a secretary was because every time I mentioned needing one, Dale shot it down. He had read somewhere, though he couldn't remember where, that 26 percent of church pastors ran off with their secretaries. Because it was in print, Dale believed it. Plus, his brother-in-law's pastor had run off with his secretary, which meant, of course, that if I had a secretary I would do the same.

"Lead us not into temptation," Dale intoned whenever I raised the subject of hiring a secretary.

*f*or as long as I had known Dale, he had taken his vacation the first week of July. Every year Dale and his wife went to the same place, Fond du Lac, Wisconsin, where they rented a cabin and fished. Dale had two bumper stickers on his car. One read, *Jesus said to them, "Follow me, and I will make you fishers…"* and the other read, *Work is for people who don't know how to fish.*

With Dale in Fond du Lac, July was the one month we got things done in the church. We saved all our important business for the July elders' meeting, which was when I brought up the subject of Harmony Friends Meeting hiring a secretary to help me write the newsletter, print the bulletins, and answer the phone.

Even with Dale gone, it was a spirited discussion. Asa Peacock mentioned that we'd never had a secretary before. Why start now?

Miriam Hodge asked if he'd had indoor plumbing growing up. Asa shook his head no.

She said, "Well, Asa, since you'd never had it, why did you bother getting it?" In one fell swoop, Miriam Hodge killed the venerable we've-never-done-it-this-way-before argument. It was a thing of beauty to behold.

Then Harvey Muldock waded in with the time-honored we-can't-afford-it argument, to which Miriam replied, "It seems a waste of money to pay Sam to do secretarial work when we could hire it done cheaper."

With all the arguments exhausted, they formed a hiring committee, and since Dale Hinshaw was gone, they appointed him to chair it.

I was the one who had to tell him. I scribbled on my to-do list, *Talk with Dale Hinshaw about sec.* I'd learned my lesson and used his full name.

Dale took it better than I thought.

He said, "I can see how having a secretary could be a help. I guess we can trust you to behave yourself."

The next week he hired a seventy-year-old secretary. His name was Frank. Frank was a widower. His wife had just died, and Dale thought making Frank our secretary would boost his spirits.

I was leery at first, but in fairness to Frank, it's worked out better than I anticipated. Frank was a bookkeeper during the Korean War, where he developed a knack for organization. Each morning he tells me my schedule. He keeps my pencils sharpened and arranges my books alphabetically. If I have a church meeting, Frank attends and takes notes. His only drawback is that he is farsighted, so he can't see well. He blames it on the war.

"It was all that squinting. But what with people getting shot at, I didn't think I should complain about not being able to see."

Some men gave their lives for freedom. Frank gave his 20/20 eyesight. He wears thick glasses that slip down his nose. He spends a lot of time looking at people over his glasses.

*I*t has been said that patience comes with age. Whoever said that never met Frank. He does not entertain fools gladly. When Fern Hampton called to complain about our worship service, Frank listened for one minute, then hung up the phone.

Complaining about the service was a weekly ritual for Fern, a deep joy, almost a sacrament. During worship she would sit in the sixth row and scribble furiously. At first I thought she was taking notes, but what she was doing was gathering evidence. She'd phone the office every Monday morning and complain for ten minutes. She'd start with the prelude and work her way through to the benediction. I used to listen to her entire harangue. After a while I learned to set the phone down, do my paperwork, then pick up the phone ten minutes later just as she was winding down.

She complains about the hymns and the sermon and about people sneaking in church announcements during prayer time. Bill Muldock is notorious for that. He stands during prayer time, bows his head, and intones, "Lord, we just ask Your blessings on our men's softball practice this Tuesday night at seven o'clock at the park." Fern glares at him from across the meeting room.

Then one Monday I wasn't at the church office, and Frank answered the phone. He listened to Fern for one minute, then hung up the phone, and she hasn't called back since.

It's like Frank told me, "Once you've been to war, you learn what's important. A good war would do wonders for Fern."

Frank has a sign over his desk that reads:

> *I can only make one person happy each day.*
> *Today is not your day.*
> *Tomorrow doesn't look good, either.*

I suspect Dale hired Frank to spite me. He thought Frank would be a burden, but that hasn't happened. People are so afraid to call the office on the off chance Frank will answer, my work load has dropped considerably.

People call and ask me to visit someone in the hospital. Frank asks them, "Why can't you go? Are your legs broken? Why do you want Pastor Sam to do your Christian work for you?"

Dale Hinshaw was the worst offender. Fearing I might have a spare moment, he would phone me daily with suggestions of things I could do. Frank put up with this for one week, then said, "Dale, if you spent as much time doing the work of the Lord as you do fishing, we'd all be better off."

*f*rank's greatest contribution to date came during the August meeting of elders. Miriam Hodge opened with prayer, read through the old business, then asked if I had anything to say.

I turned to Frank and asked him to read my to-do list. Frank squinted at the list through his thick glasses.

"It says here you to need to talk with Dale Hinshaw about sex," he said.

The room grew quiet. The elders raised their eyes and looked down the table at Dale, wondering why Dale needed to be talked to about sex. What had he done? Was there something they needed to know?

I asked Frank to hand me the to-do list.

"No, Frank, it says for me to talk with Dale about a secretary. I abbreviated the word *secretary*. That's *s-e-c*, not *s-e-x*. I needed to talk with Dale about a secretary."

Dale looked vastly relieved.

Frank said, "Maybe you ought to talk with Dale about sex just the same. Everyone's talking about sex these days, except for the church. Maybe that's why we're so messed up about sex. The people who should be teaching about it, aren't. Maybe we ought to teach about sex."

Then he paused and said, "Golly, I sure miss sex. I miss the holding part."

Dale reddened and Miriam blushed. I was relatively certain that in our hundred and seventy years of existence, sex had never been the focus of an elder's meeting at Harmony Friends Meeting.

Dale sat bolt upright and said, "I think Frank is right. Someone needs to talk about sex to our teenagers. Just the other day I saw two of our kids kissing in the church parking lot. Pastor, why don't you talk with those kids?"

Frank said, "Dale, how come you want Pastor Sam to do everything? Why can't you talk with the teenagers?"

So that's how Dale Hinshaw came to talk with the youth of Harmony Friends Meeting about the birds and the bees.

The next Sunday, Dale and his wife came to church armed with pictures of flowers, of pistils and stamens. He spoke at length about pollination. Then he asked if there were any questions. There weren't.

Dale reported back to the September meeting of elders. He said, "Well, I got them squared around. We won't be having any sex problems in this church. You can bet on that."

Frank asked him what he had talked about, specifically. He wanted details.

Dale said, "Pistils and stamens. They got the message."

Frank asked, "Did you tell them about the holding part? How the holding part is the best. How it's sweeter over the years. How they need to wait until they're married. That when love and commitment aren't in it, it'll leave you feeling empty and cheap. Did you tell them that?"

Dale said he implied it.

Frank erupted, "Good golly, man, you got to put the hay down where the goats can get it."

That's when Frank volunteered to talk with the youth of Harmony Friends Meeting about the birds and the bees.

I went with him. He didn't bring any pictures of flowers or pistils and stamens. Mostly, he just talked. He talked about his wife Martha, and how they met, and how tempted they had been, and how they waited. He spoke of how he missed her during the war, how he kept her picture in his shirt pocket, next to his heart. He hung his head and wiped his eyes and told how much he missed her now. Then he told them sex was a gift of love from God and that's what made it sacred. And how it's our job not to cheapen it.

Then he asked if the kids had any questions.

One boy raised his hand and asked if it was all right to pick flowers from a neighbor's garden.

Frank asked him what that had to do with sex. The boy wasn't sure, but that's what Dale had told him—not to pick flowers from your neighbor's garden.

Well, that's how things get done in this place. We put things off and put things off until someone like Frank gets fed up and wades in and gets the job done. And if that doesn't work, we wait until Dale Hinshaw goes fishing, then we do it.

But there are some things that shouldn't wait, things we need to talk about right now. Making sure our children know right from wrong and good from bad is one of them. I wrote it on my to-do list: *Talk with your sons about sex.*

Dale lent me his pistil and stamen pictures. Frank said if I had any questions, he'd be happy to help.

By golly, Dale Hinshaw was right. If you hire a church secretary, sex is never far behind.

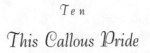
Ten

This Callous Pride

O f all the things I like about summer, what I like most is that we don't hold Sunday school. It wasn't my idea—it's been that way as long as I can remember.

The Sunday before Memorial Day we hold a Sunday school picnic after meeting. Each class does a recitation. It's the same every year. The children sing "Jesus Loves Me," though in watching them you certainly couldn't fault Jesus if He found some of them easier to love than others. The ladies of the Mary and Martha Sunday school class recite a poem, and Bob Miles Sr., who teaches the Live Free or Die class, leads everyone in the Pledge of Allegiance. He stands on a picnic table, leads the pledge, then advises the rest of us where the food line starts, even though we've been lining up the same way since 1964 and could do it in our sleep.

The picnic tables are set up behind the meetinghouse, underneath the trees, alongside the parking lot. The line forms at the basketball goal, which Dale Hinshaw wants to take down so the teenagers will hang out somewhere else. The women of the Mary and Martha class are first in line, then the men of the Live Free or Die class, then the families with children, then the teenagers—who eat fast then shoot Horse at the basketball goal.

It requires no special skill to stand in line, so no one listens to Bob Sr., which infuriates him. He wants the church to buy a bullhorn so he can be heard. He brings it up every May when we're planning the Sunday school picnic. Says the same thing every year.

"It's not just for the picnic. We could use it for other things. If there was civil disorder and we had to crack down, a bullhorn would come in handy."

Bob Sr. is intrigued with the idea of the town falling into chaos and the townspeople begging him to restore order.

We tell him if he wants a bullhorn, he'll have to buy it with his own money. He says, "You'll be sorry. One day this town will erupt. It happened in Los Angeles. There's no reason it couldn't happen here. Trust me, this town is a powder keg. And when it blows, you'll wish you had a bullhorn."

He talks about it during Sunday school, too, which is why I welcome the summer reprieve. He talks about how America is going to pot, how young people aren't worth a darn, how folks don't pull together anymore, and how everyone is lazy. His answer to moral depravity is a bullhorn.

Bob Miles Sr. founded the Live Free or Die Sunday school class in 1960. Concerned about the impending Communist threat and how President Kennedy was put into office by the pope, he began the class as a watchdog group to guard against foreign infiltration at Harmony Friends Meeting. In 1960, when Nikita Khrushchev visited a pig farm in Iowa, Bob Sr. drove ten hours to hold up a sign that read *LIVE FREE OR DIE*. There was a picture in *Time* magazine of Nikita Krushchev lifting up a pig, and right behind him, Bob Sr. with his sign. Then Bob came home and the very next Sunday began the Live Free or Die class.

It is not the kind of class that attracts the current generation, who, while valuing freedom, are more interested in parenting classes and classes on biblical financial management. Bob Sr.'s class is fading, which he laments at least once a month during open worship. We sit in silence waiting for the Lord to speak, and Bob Sr. rises to his feet to warn against Communism. He writes letters to the *Herald* every week which his son, Bob Jr., who does not share his father's political philosophy, refuses to print.

But Bob Sr. is persistent. If the *Herald* won't print his opinion, he'll offer it during church, when no one can stop him, though not for lack of trying.

This past May, during the elders' meeting, Miriam Hodge suggested naming Bob Sr. as our Official Prayer Warrior.

I thought it unwise. I thought it ill-advised to give Bob Sr. a platform. I imagined him rising to his feet during worship and ordering us to pray for a return to the gold standard.

But Miriam was one step ahead of me. "We'll make him our Official Prayer Warrior," she said, "but we'll have him pray according to Scripture."

She opened her Bible to the Gospel of Matthew and read from chapter 6, "When you pray, go into your closet and shut the door and pray to your Father who is in secret; and your Father who sees in secret will reward you."

Miriam said, "The only closet in the meetinghouse is down in the basement, next to the furnace. We can put him down there on Sunday mornings. He'll be out of our hair."

Bob Miles Sr., banished to the utility closet. A glorious thought.

That Sunday we asked him to be our Official Prayer Warrior. We could see he was intrigued with the idea of being named a warrior.

Then Miriam said, "Of course, if you're our Official Prayer Warrior, you'll have to pray according to Scripture."

"What do you mean?" Bob asked. She quoted from Matthew and told him he'd have to pray in the closet down in the basement.

I could see Bob begin to waver.

"Of course," I told him, "we'll need to put in the bulletin that you're the Official Prayer Warrior."

It was then Bob Sr. felt called to the ministry of prayer.

The next Sunday he went downstairs to the utility closet, closed the door behind him, and sat on a folding chair next to the furnace. We sang our hymns, I preached my sermon without fear of rebuttal, then we settled into silence so the Lord could speak. People were relaxed. This was wonderful. We didn't have to worry about Bob rising to his feet and wading in. Oh, such quiet joy. One minute passed, then two.

Peace, perfect peace.

It was then we heard Bob's voice rising up through the heating vents.

"OH, LORD, THESE ARE A STIFF-NECKED PEOPLE WHO SCORN TRUTH. STRIKE THEM DOWN IN THEIR INSOLENCE. BREAK THEIR HAUGHTY SPIRITS."

He went on and on. We could hear each word. The heating ducts serving as a kind of bullhorn.

Bob prayed for fifteen minutes. He beseeched the Lord to chasten us. He railed against the Communist threat. He prophesied against the New World Order and Democrats and bar codes.

Jessie Peacock, who sat over the furnace, pounded the floor with her foot. Bob prayed even louder.

"BRING THEM TO THEIR KNEES, LORD," and "WOE TO YOU, HYPOCRITES!"

It was John the Baptist come to life.

Finally, he stopped. I prayed a closing prayer—loud, so Bob Sr. would know church was over.

Bob came upstairs. Miriam Hodge and I met him at the front door.

Miriam said, "Bob, we had in mind you'd sort of whisper your prayers."

Bob Sr. drew himself up and stared at Miriam and said, "Warriors don't whisper." And he walked out the door.

*T*he next week was the Sunday before Memorial Day. We held our Sunday school picnic. The kids sang "Jesus Loves Me." The Mary and Martha class read a poem. Then Bob Sr. climbed up on a picnic table, cleared his throat, and led us in the Pledge of Allegiance. As it wound to a close, he made us repeat it.

"This time," he ordered, "say it like you mean it."

Then he said that, as the Official Prayer Warrior, he had something to say. He spoke of the sacrifice of the veterans, and how we Quakers tarnished their memories by being pacifists.

"This pacifism stuff," he declared, "makes us look like Communists. What would happen if everyone was a pacifist?"

Asa Peacock didn't realize it was a rhetorical question. "Peace," he ventured.

Bob Sr. went on. Ranting against evolution and the United Nations and various Hollywood liberals.

After five minutes, I interrupted Bob to say the meal grace.

We filled our plates, then stood in line as Fern Hampton and the women of the Friendly Women's Circle poured weak lemonade into Styrofoam cups. I took my food and my family and sat with Miriam and Ellis Hodge.

We talked about Bob Sr.

"I've created a monster," Miriam said. "I never should have made him the Official Prayer Warrior."

Ellis patted her hand. "Don't be so hard on yourself, honey," he told her. "Bob was a jerk long before that."

The attendance was down the next Sunday. People were tired of Bob Sr. Tired of sitting in the silence and listening to his prayers rise up through the heat vents. I couldn't blame them. Life is hard enough without being prayed against. I knew the time had come to speak with him. I couldn't bear the thought of it. I hated conflict. I liked peace and quiet; that's why I was a Quaker. But it had to be done.

I went to Bob's house the next evening after supper. I rang his doorbell. It played the first two lines of the national anthem.

> *Oh, say can you see, by the dawn's early light,*
> *What so proudly we hailed at the twilight's last gleaming?*

I could hear Bob Sr. singing the words inside the house. He swung open the door.

I greeted him, walked inside, and sat on the couch.

There was a picture of George Washington in his living room, over the television. George Washington giving his painful smile, like he'd stubbed his toe and was trying hard not to cuss.

All the way over, I had wondered how best to approach Bob. I decided to go with straightforward. I dreaded it, but this was no time for subtlety.

I said, "Bob Miles, your behavior has been rude, and we're tired of it. You disrupt our worship with your prayers against us. You're acting like a spoiled child who hasn't gotten his way. If you don't straighten up, you can't be the Official Prayer Warrior."

He rocked back in his chair and stared. He'd never been talked to this way.

He got ready to say something, but I didn't let him. I went on. "You want everyone to do things your way, and when they don't, you throw a fit. You talk about how this is the land of the free, but you really don't want anyone to be free. You want everything your way. And that makes you a tyrant."

I didn't stay to hear his response. I was too afraid. I stood and walked out the door, went home, and went to bed. I lay there feeling guilty, wondering if I'd been too hard. I shouldn't have called him a tyrant. Just because something is true doesn't mean it has to be said. I didn't sleep much.

When I got to my office the next morning, Bob was waiting for me. He was mad, I could tell. He said he wouldn't be coming back to church. My first thought was to talk him out of it, to tell him he was welcome to stay. Then I came to my senses and recognized Bob's departure for what it was—a gift from the Lord. So I kept quiet except to say, "Well, Bob, that is up to you. You are free to do that."

I phoned Miriam Hodge to tell her.

"He'll be back," she said. "We won't get off that easy."

But he didn't come that Sunday and hasn't been back since.

I felt bad about it at first, though ours is a sweeter fellowship without him. You try to win people over with love and patience, but some people don't want to be won over. All they want is to get their way.

I saw Bob Sr. several times over the summer, at the Coffee Cup Restaurant. I'd smile and hold out my hand, but he wouldn't take it. I invited him back to church. No thank you, he'd say. Then I got a phone call from the Baptist minister. He was telling me Bob wanted to transfer his membership to their church. He asked what Bob was like.

"Interesting," I told him.

I wish it hadn't come to this. I wish we could have softened him. We tried for eighty years, but failed. Now we're giving the Baptists a crack at him. May God bless and guide them.

He might come back. Miriam Hodge said it's happened once before. "It was during Vietnam," she said. "He read a story about Quakers protesting the war and it set him off, but he came back. Don't worry, he'll be back."

I told her I wasn't worried.

But I am worried. I fear for his soul. I worry how God can tame such a hard and bitter pride. This callous pride, which shuts first the ear and then the heart.

With Bob Sr. gone, the Live Free or Die class is looking for someone to lead the pledge at the Sunday school picnic next year. They asked me if I could do it.

"Do I have to stand on the picnic table?" I asked.

"Sam," they said, "stand where you feel led."

In the end, that is what we all must do. Stand where we feel led. Stand straight, stand tall, and try hard to remember that other folks might be led to stand elsewhere.

Eleven

The Aluminum Years

On the third page of *The Harmony Herald,* opposite the editorial page, is the "Years Past" column. Every week, Bob Miles Jr. sorts through the boxes of old issues of the *Herald* and reprints articles from ten, twenty-five, and fifty years ago.

Because I prefer what has been to what will be, the "Years Past" column is the first thing I read when the *Herald* lands on my doorstep. The past is my sitting at Grandma's table eating rhubarb pie, with Grandma hovering over me, spooning another piece on my plate. The future is the bank repossessing my house and me having to take my family to live with my spinster aunt in the next town over. So I love opening the *Herald* and backing up twenty-five years.

The first week of August I was reading the "Twenty-five Years Ago This Week" section about when I was a child and the Harmony Little League All-Stars won the state championship. It all came back—how that September the All-Stars had paraded down Main Street, riding on a float in the Corn and Sausage Days Parade, just behind the Sausage Queen, with Bob Miles Sr. snapping their picture and running it on the front page of the *Herald.*

Twenty-five years later, Bob Miles Jr. reprinted the picture. Skinny boys with big ears and buzz haircuts. The boys were my age—I knew them all—and though I had played Little League I hadn't made the All-Star team. I was extremely farsighted. My mother wouldn't let me wear my glasses for fear they would break. I would stand in the outfield and squint toward home plate, praying for God to direct the ball away from me.

The other players on our team would crouch and yell "Hey batter, hey batter, hey batter…" They sounded like crickets. I never yelled because I didn't want the attention. I didn't want the batter to sense my presence and hit the ball my way. I would watch the pitcher wind up and hurl the ball. I could see the ball leave the bat. I could see it sail through the air in a high arc. I could hear Coach Kennedy yelling at me to catch it, but as the ball came closer I'd lose sight of it. I would stab my hand in the air, and more often than not, the ball would strike me in the head. After a while, I learned to drop to the ground and cover my head whenever the coach called my name. This saved my head but wrecked my chance to play on the All-Star team.

*N*ow, twenty-five Augusts later, it is a slow news month. We sit on our porches and drink iced tea and don't generate much news. The only thing for Bob Jr. to write about is the heat, which we already know about. So Bob ran an extended version of the "Years Past" column. I read it in reverse, starting with fifty years ago, then twenty-five, then ten. I got to the "Ten Years Ago This Week" section. There was my name: "Samuel Addison Gardner and Barbara Ann Griffith were joined in holy matrimony this past Saturday…"

I stopped reading. I counted back on my fingers. A panic gripped me. My tenth anniversary was the next day and I had forgotten it.

I heard the phone ring, heard my wife yell that she would answer it.

I could hear her talking, faintly. "Yes, it's ten years tomorrow, but I think Sam's forgotten. I'm not saying anything. I'm just going to wait and see what happens."

I had not done well with anniversaries. On our fifth anniversary, which was the "wood" anniversary, I went to the lumberyard and bought two wooden posts and built Barbara a clothesline and gift-wrapped some wooden clothespins, which I thought was a creative gift. I thought everyone liked clotheslines and falling to sleep on line-dried sheets. I was wrong.

On our sixth anniversary I gave her a personalized license plate with her initials, which spelled out the word *BAG,* which did not occur to me until I took her by the hand and walked her outside with her eyes closed. I positioned her in front of the car and said, "Okay, you can open your eyes now."

Barbara opened her eyes and looked at the license plate, then at me, then back at the license plate. I could see her lips move. "Bag," she was saying. Then she turned to me and said, "I didn't think you could do worse than the clothesline. I was wrong."

Now our tenth anniversary was one day away and I had nothing planned. I called a gift shop in the city to find out what to buy for tenth anniversaries. I couldn't call the local store. They knew my voice. They'd say, "Is that you, Sam Gardner? Why are you just now asking?" and it would get back to my wife. There is no privacy in this town. Your stupidity is laid bare for all to see.

Since my fifth anniversary, gift giving had grown more complicated. The saleslady told me I could choose between giving a traditional gift or buying a modern gift. The traditional gift for tenth anniversaries was aluminum. Aluminum was within my budget. I liked that. The modern gift, the lady told me, was diamond jewelry. I didn't care for that at all. I wondered who changed it.

I'm a traditionalist. I don't do something just because it's a fad. I went with aluminum. I bought Barbara ten cans of diet soda in aluminum cans. One can for each year. I gift wrapped each one. She'd like that, unwrapping ten separate gifts. She'd think it was creative.

That night as we lay in bed, she asked, "Should I make plans for tomorrow, or did you maybe have a little something in mind?"

"Nothing special," I told her. "Just another day. Got to go to the office, then do some visitation. But I'll be home for supper. Could you maybe make some of that good meat loaf you make? We haven't had that in a while."

It was dark in our bedroom. I couldn't see her face, but I could hear her let out a sigh, then a snort. It was resignation working its way toward anger. I couldn't wait for the next day. Wouldn't she be surprised! Ten cans of diet soda. What a fun surprise!

*W*hen I woke up the next morning, Barbara was gone. There was a note on the table saying she'd gone for a walk. A long walk. She had underlined the word *long* and had pressed down hard with the pencil. I could see where the lead had broken.

I waited for her to get home. I heard her in the kitchen. She was standing at the sink. She turned to face me, and I held out a wrapped can. She smiled a big, pretty smile, then hugged me and said, "You remembered."

"Of course I remembered," I told her. "I'd never forget our anniversary."

She unwrapped it, then looked at me.

I smiled. "Aluminum," I told her. "The tenth year is the aluminum year. Isn't that great? I got you ten of them. Get it? Ten cans of soda for ten years of marriage. Isn't that great?"

She didn't say anything. She unwrapped the other cans. She was working her way from resignation toward anger. She got to the last can. That was the can I'd taped the diamond ring to. When we'd married, I didn't have enough money for a diamond ring. When she agreed to marry me, I promised her that someday I'd buy her one.

She'd told me, "You don't have to. It wouldn't make us any more married. I'm not marrying you for a ring." Which made me want to buy it for her all the more.

A couple years after we married, my grandmother died and left me two thousand dollars. I put it in the bank. It was our emergency money. It was money for desperate times. With our tenth anniversary only one day away, I was desperate. I took the money and drove to the city and bought the ring.

Barbara unwrapped the last can. The ring was taped to the top, bright and shiny.

She began to weep. This beautiful woman who had worked to put me through school, who had borne our children, who had told me she liked the license plate after all and had taken it off the car when we'd sold it and bolted it to our new car.

"Times have changed," I told her. "The traditional tenth anniversary gift was aluminum. But the modern gift is diamond jewelry. You know me, I like to keep up with the times."

*L*ate that afternoon I went up to the attic and looked through the boxes for the champagne glasses from our wedding day. It took two hours to find them. It was August-hot. I called my mother to tell her that she wanted to take her grandchildren for the night. I washed the champagne glasses and took a shower and put on my suit. Barbara was out at the clothesline. I called her into the house.

She walked in, wiping the sweat from her brow. I handed her a champagne glass of diet soda.

"It's can number one," I told her. "I've heard it's a good year." Then I kissed her. Then we did something else, on which I won't elaborate because I'm a traditionalist.

Afterwards, we talked. She said, "You're a piece of work, Sam Gardner. I had my doubts about you, especially after the clothesline and the license plate, but you're doing better."

I told her when you've been hit in the head with a baseball as many times as I have, it takes a while to get over it.

I love my wife. I can't believe she chose me. Growing up, no one ever chose me for anything. We would pick teams for baseball, and the captains would argue over me.

"You take him."

"No, you take him."

I would stand, squinty eyed, staring at the ground, digging at the dirt with the toe of my shoe.

Then I went to college and met my wife. She sat next to me in the dining hall. I thought maybe she'd lost a bet and that sitting with me was the penalty. The next day she sat by me again, so I asked her name.

"Barbara," she told me.

"That's a pretty name," I said.

"It means *stranger*," she confided.

Sitting there, looking at her, I felt smooth and witty. I said, "Hello, stranger. Pleased to meet you. My name is Sam," I told her. "It means *one who listens.*"

So we sat together and she talked and I listened.

I still can't believe she married me. I look up from the pulpit and see her in the fifth row, just behind Miriam and Ellis Hodge. I watch her push her hair behind her ears, how it sweeps over her shoulders. Watch her eyes. She has one blue eye and one brown eye. People look at her and suspect something is a little different, but can't quite put their finger on it. As a child, it made her self-conscious.

S he isn't perfection, but then I've never been drawn to perfection. When I was twelve years old and watched the All-Stars riding in the Corn and Sausage Days Parade, I saw how perfection went to their heads. It ruined them. Fifteen boys who, before perfection visited them, were easily tolerated—but in perfection became unbearable. Having tasted perfection so young, they assumed perfection would be their life's pattern and have been disappointed ever since.

But since I was acquainted with failure from an early age, I made my peace with it and am pleasantly surprised when life goes well. Ten years in a wonderful marriage, with two healthy sons. It shocks me to think of it. So blessed.

It is easy, in these aluminum years, to believe in a loving God. It's the only thing that makes sense. It isn't skill and pluck and hard work that get us where we are. It's grace, nothing else.

It's God, pointing the divine finger our way, saying, "You there, with the squinty eyes, digging your toes in the dirt, it's *you* I want."

Sometimes I feel like I'm sitting at God's table and I've just finished one piece of blessing, and God smiles and says, "Here, Sam, have another."

That's how it feels. That's exactly how it feels.

Twelve

Brother Norman and the Bus

As far back as I can remember, Dale Hinshaw has been an elder at Harmony Friends Meeting, even though the rules say you can serve only six years. You serve six years, then are paroled, having done your time. But Dale keeps volunteering, and we keep letting him, even though some of our most half-witted decisions can be traced back to Dale Hinshaw—including the decision to buy a used bus from a rock band and use it as a church bus.

The group was named Venom. They wore leather pants and went without shirts and had rattlesnakes tattooed on their chests. They writhed on the stage and hissed at the audience. It was hard to make out the words to their songs, except for the cuss words, which they spoke loudly and clearly and often. No one mistook them for a gospel quartet.

Venom was driving through Harmony when their bus broke down. It was towed to Harvey Muldock's garage. It took Harvey two weeks to get the parts, by which time the members of Venom were gone, to the great relief of our town. Harvey Muldock was telling about their bus during an elders' meeting, which was when Dale Hinshaw suggested the church buy the bus for the cost of the repairs—three hundred dollars.

"We could take the money from our missions fund. It could be the start of our bus ministry," he said. "We could drive to the nursing home and bring the people in. We can use it for mission trips. The devil has had that bus long enough. Let's see what the Lord can do with it."

So that's what they did.

Dale painted it himself, with a paintbrush. Royal blue. On the sides of the bus he painted the church name, and on the back he painted *Follow Me to Harmony Friends Meeting!*

Now the paint is faded, and if you look closely you can make out the word *Venom* and the faint outline of a rattlesnake. The bus was used two Sundays before it broke down again. We now understand why the members of Venom never bothered to come back for it. This was five years ago, and the bus still sits in the meetinghouse parking lot, a monument to shallow thinking.

There is one window in my office. When Dale Hinshaw parked the bus five years ago, he parked it right in front of the window. The next Sunday the bus wouldn't start, and it's sat there ever since. Instead of looking out at sky, I look at the bus. It is a strong discouragement.

One Monday morning, late in August, I was sitting in the office reading the newsletter from the Quaker headquarters. The front page was the superintendent's letter. He believes in the power of words, that we are one newsletter article away from vitality. He uses nouns as verbs and writes about impacting the world and visioning our objectives and imaging our destiny. He reveres numbers. There are newsletter articles about "Eight Ways to Impact Our World!!" and "Ten Steps to Visioning Our Objectives!!" He makes extensive use of the exclamation point and bold print.

On the next page were the prayer requests. I scanned the list. Prayers for our leaders. Prayers for various sick people. Then, there it was:

"Prayers for Brother Norman as he ministers to the Choctaw Indians!! Needs transportation for youth programs!!!"

Brother Norman was a nice guy, but not the brightest bulb in the chandelier. When he'd graduated from seminary, no church would have him, so our superintendent talked with him about impacting the world as a missionary to the Choctaw Indians and sent him to Oklahoma, where Brother Norman began a building program.

Each month Brother Norman wrote the Quaker headquarters to report his prayer needs. Electricians one month, plumbers the next. Before long, the meetinghouse was built. Now he was praying for a bus to transport the Choctaw youth.

I raised my eyes from the newsletter and peered out my office window. The tires were dry-rotted and stuck to the pavement. The bus wouldn't start, but Harvey Muldock could fix it.

The week before, I had suggested that the men of the church needed a ministry. Dale Hinshaw had proposed a baseball ministry. His idea was to repair the bus and drive to the ball games in the city and invite other men from the town to join us. Then on the way home to Harmony, we could witness to them.

He had come across this strategy in the Quaker newsletter. It was idea number four in the "Eight Ways to Impact Our World!!" article.

Dale said, "We'll have them right there on the bus. They'll have to listen. We'll drive slow and wear 'em down." Dale thought the gospel was not compelling in and of itself, that people needed to be coerced into believing it.

I suggested donating the bus to the fire department so they could burn it for the practice. Or maybe towing it to the county fair and charging people a dollar to hit it with a sledge hammer. Better yet, we could sell it to a rock band.

I said, "The Lord has put up with this bus long enough. Let's give it back to the devil."

Then, the very next Monday morning, I read the Quaker newsletter about Brother Norman and the Choctaw youth in need of transportation.

I called Brother Norman on the phone to tell him his prayers had been answered. Then I phoned Harvey Muldock, who towed the bus to his garage. It took a couple weeks, but he got it running. Dale sanded off the snake and *Follow Me to Harmony Friends Meeting!* and the word *Venom*. He painted the bus red, with a paint brush.

I walked over to Dale's house to see it.

"It needs a Scripture passage," he said. "Something that might bring people to the Lord if they happen to glance at it. I've narrowed it down to two verses—John 10:14 about the good shepherd, or Revelation 13:16 about the mark of the beast."

"I've always been partial to John 10:14," I told him.

Dale frowned. "I was leaning toward Revelation," he said.

"Let's flip a coin," I suggested. "Heads I win, tails you lose."

"Fair enough," Dale said.

I flipped the coin. It was heads.

"You win," Dale said.

"Then we'll go with John 10:14," I declared.

So that's what he painted down the side of the bus: *I am the Good Shepherd; I know my own and my own know me.*

A fine Scripture.

That Sunday I announced from the pulpit that Dale and Harvey and I would be driving the bus to Oklahoma. After church, the Friendly Women's Circle surrounded the bus and prayed for our safe journey as we went forth onto the mission field. Then they counted out six hundred dollars into Dale's hands, money they'd raised at their annual Chicken Noodle Dinner. Six hundred dollars! Cash!

"You be sure Brother Norman gets that money," Fern Hampton warned him. "Don't be spending it on wild living."

I looked at Dale in his plaid shirt, seed corn cap, and orthopedic shoes. He didn't strike me as a candidate for wild living.

We left for Oklahoma the next day. By late afternoon we were crossing the Mississippi River into St. Louis. There was the Gateway Arch, rising up from the west bank of the river. We'd never seen it before except on television when the St. Louis Cardinals played.

Dale was driving. "Let's stop," he said. He veered the bus across four lanes of traffic and just made the exit.

We parked the bus, went into the Arch and rode the elevator all the way to the top. We crowded against the windows. We could see all of St. Louis, including the baseball stadium. It was beautiful, like an emerald. We felt like angels looking down from heaven. We could see the groundskeepers rolling the diamond. A trickle of ant people was moving into the seats.

Harvey said, "I think there's a game today."

A man standing next to us said, "That's right. The Cardinals and the Cubbies. Mark McGwire's going for the home run record. Number sixty-two."

We climbed back in the bus and drove past the stadium. There was a man out front scalping tickets. He held up three tickets and yelled, "Six hundred dollars!" which we took to be a sign from the Lord.

Harvey said, "You know, we could pay it back. The Friendly Women would never know. We could write Brother Norman a check. Wouldn't that be something to see the record home run hit? My father was there in 1961 when Roger Maris set his record, and he never forgot it. Whenever we'd watch a ball game, he'd say, 'Did I ever tell you about the time I saw Roger Maris hit number sixty-one?' Then he'd talk about that ball sailing over the fence. He never forgot it. He talked about it on his deathbed, about seeing that."

Dale said, "We'd be a witness to history. We'd never forget it. Then we could drive through the night and be at Brother Norman's in the morning."

So that's what we did. We bought the tickets and found our seats.

It was a hot evening. The late sun beat down, right on us. A vendor walked down our aisle.

"Cold beer," he yelled. "Get your cold beer."

It was unmercifully hot.

I looked at Dale and Harvey. "I drank a beer once. I was in college. It didn't taste bad, either."

Dale said, "I haven't had a beer since I became a Christian."

Harvey said, "You know, the apostle Paul once advised Timothy to refresh himself with an adult beverage."

Dale declared, "I know that verse. The Epistle of 1 Timothy. Chapter 5. Verse 23."

I could feel the sweat trickle down my back and into my underwear.

It was cruelly hot, and what was one beer? That was no big sin, was it? Harvey yelled at the vendor and held up three fingers and passed our money down the row. Back came three beers. We sat in our seats and watched the game and sipped our beers. It was such a thrill, getting away with something.

Then Mark McGwire came to bat and the crowd grew still. It was like church. Like the silence after the first hymn when we're waiting for the Lord to inspire us. It was that kind of quiet. The pitcher glanced at first base, then at third base, then reared back and hurled the ball toward home plate. Mark McGwire brought the bat around, it was in slow motion, and we heard a *crack!* and that little white ball sailed over the fence and into the crowd.

Everyone in the country was watching their television sets—even the people in Harmony. So when the camera swept the roaring crowd and paused on us, standing and holding our beers, people from

Harmony said, "I thought they were on a mission trip. What are they doing there? I thought they were in Oklahoma with Brother Norman and the Choctaw youth. And what is that they're drinking? That doesn't look like soda to me."

Before long it was all over town. Everyone knew, including our wives. Some of the men in the church wondered why they hadn't been invited on the mission trip, and weren't too happy about being left out.

*A*fter the game, we climbed on the bus and drove through the night, talking of Mark McGwire's home run and how we'd never forget it.

"I can't wait till we get home," Dale said. "Won't it be fun telling people we were there?"

Harvey said, "Dale, don't you dare say a word about being there. If those Friendly Women find out we were at the game, they'll kill us."

That smothered our elation. We'd seen history made and couldn't brag. What a bitter disappointment.

Early the next morning we pulled up in the church parking lot and sounded the horn. Brother Norman was waiting with the Choctaw youth.

"We were expecting you last night," Brother Norman said.

"We stopped to do some birdwatching," Harvey told him. "Saw some lovely cardinals."

Brother Norman smiled. "Isn't it nice to enjoy God's creation?"

"It's wonderful," Harvey agreed. "Simply wonderful."

Brother Norman and the Choctaw youth walked around the bus, admiring it. Brother Norman read the Scripture verse Dale had painted: *I am the Good Shepherd; I know my own and my own know me.*

"A fine Scripture," he said.

"It wasn't my first choice," Dale allowed.

Brother Norman showed us the meetinghouse: the red carpet, the bathroom, his office, the folding wooden chairs with the Bible racks on back, the Choctaw youth room with a Ping-Pong table and beanbag chairs. So proud of his ministry.

Dale took pictures. "This'll make a fine slide show," he said. Dale felt called to the ministry of slide shows.

Harvey said, "Brother Norman, you're doing a fine work here. We'll be sure to tell the folks back in Harmony all about it. Oh, by the way, we wanted you to have this." He pulled a check for $600 from his pocket and handed it to Brother Norman.

Brother Norman beamed. Then Harvey said it was time to leave, that we'd done what we came to do.

I remember that moment distinctly, how each of us thought the very same thought at the very same time. It was the thought that while we had given careful attention to getting to Oklahoma, we had given no thought whatsoever to getting home.

Harvey said, "Maybe we can call one of our wives. Maybe one of them can come get us."

We crowded into Brother Norman's office to use the phone. Harvey dialed his house. His wife answered. Harvey didn't do much talking. Mostly he listened, though every now and then we could hear him ask a question.

"Game?" he asked. "What game?" He was trying to sound indignant. "Cardinals and Cubs? Did they play?... You say you saw us there? Well, you know people look different on television. Television does that to people. Makes you look like someone else." Then he said, "Well, after forty years of marriage, I'm just sorry you don't trust me more." He sniffed as he said it, sounding hurt.

That's when Harvey's wife said she was too busy to come get us, that maybe we could stay with Brother Norman for a few days and learn what it meant to be Christian.

Dale and I called our wives, who offered similar suggestions and, coincidentally, were also very busy.

That night we slept in the Choctaw youth room, on the beanbag chairs.

The next morning, Brother Norman offered to drive us home. We piled into his car and headed toward Harmony. Brother Norman drove. I sat behind him, staring at his thinning hair through Oklahoma and into Missouri. He talked about the Choctaws and how much he loved being where he was.

"I'm the most blessed man you'll ever meet," he told us.

We rolled into St. Louis. I looked to my left and saw the stadium where we'd been two days before.

I was struck with a happy thought.

"Now that people know we went to the game, we'll be able to talk about seeing Mark McGwire hit his home run," I said.

Dale and Harvey brightened.

We crossed the Mississippi River and started into Illinois. I contemplated Brother Norman's neck. It looked like a road map. Thin, wrinkled roads running all directions. His shirt collar, frayed and worn. Years ago we'd sent him to the Choctaws, presuming he had nothing to offer us. But what he had to offer was what we needed most of all—simple faith. Though we didn't know that, and sent him away.

We pulled into Harmony as night was falling. My wife and boys were sitting on the front porch, waiting for me.

My wife wasn't mad anymore.

"What was it like?" she asked.

I recounted my trip, telling them about Mark McGwire and Brother Norman.

Then we fell quiet, listening to the crickets.

After a time, my wife took our boys upstairs to brush their teeth and put them down. I stayed on the porch, thinking. Thinking how we're so busy cheering the Mark McGwires, we overlook the Brother Normans. This steady man who looks to the Good Shepherd. Follows Him right down the road in his bright red bus. Never straying, always praying. Impacting the world! Visioning his objectives! Imaging his destiny!

Never hitting a home run, but every day advancing the runners.

Fall

Thirteen

First Grade

When I was growing up, the kids in town pedaled their bicycles or walked to school, which they still do. The kids in the country ride one of the fourteen school buses, all of which are driven by members of the Lefter family, who cornered the Harmony bus-driving market before I was born and have been at it ever since.

Morey Lefter, who was the kingpin of the Lefter bus cartel, began driving in 1949 and drove for forty-six years. In 1989, Bob Miles Jr. took Morey's picture for the *Herald* to commemorate his driving one million nearly accident-free miles. The only blemish on his record happened in 1974 when Morey backed into Fern Hampton's brand-new Lincoln Town Car which was parked in the teachers' parking lot.

We did not hold that against Morey. It was the consensus of the town that Morey was simply the vehicle for God's judgment. It bothered us to see a civil servant driving a luxury car, and we thought Morey was simply being prophetic. Shortly afterward, Fern traded in the Lincoln Town Car for a Chevrolet Impala, and after a few years the Lincoln was forgotten by most of us, though some still hold it against her. Every now and then someone at Harmony Friends Meeting stands in the silence and talks about the beauty of simplicity and laments how simplicity is a dying tradition. Then they turn and frown at Fern, even though the Lincoln was twenty-five years ago and she's driven Chevys ever since.

Fern Hampton was my first-grade teacher. It is the Quaker custom to avoid the use of titles such as Mr. or Mrs. or Doctor or Reverend among our membership. We believe that all are equal at the foot of the cross. Titles confer an honor which belongs solely to the Lord. That is what my mother taught me. So when I was a small child, Fern Hampton was introduced to me as Fern Hampton and that is what I called her.

I would sit in the fifth pew and turn around during the greeting time and say, "Hello, Fern Hampton," and offer my hand. She would reply, "Good morning, Sam Gardner," and shake my hand.

Then I went to first grade and she was my teacher. I walked into her classroom the first day of school and said, "Hello, Fern Hampton," just like I did at meeting.

She looked up from her desk and said, "While we are at school, you are to address me as Mrs. Hampton."

That's when I knew she wasn't a true Quaker, that she left her Quaker principles at the door of the meetinghouse. The Lincoln Town Car only confirmed my suspicions. So when Morey Lefter backed into her Town Car and broke off the hood ornament, I reasoned that it was not unlike the Old Testament prophets tearing down false idols and I quietly rejoiced.

I remember what my mother had taught me, that the Lord lifts up the lowly and casts down the haughty. I was only in the first grade and had already witnessed the sure justice of the Almighty.

I believed that calling Fern Hampton "Mrs. Hampton" was a test from the Lord, and that holy obedience required me to call her "Fern Hampton" no matter what she said. So I called her "Fern

Hampton," only to find myself face to face with the principal, who rewarded my faith with a paddling. I bent over and grabbed my ankles and thought of Jesus on the cross, suffering for Truth, and I felt a proud thrill. One, two, three whacks, all of them hard, and I didn't even cry. Instead, I felt honored to suffer for the One True Faith.

Not only had Fern Hampton violated the Quaker standards of equality and simplicity, she had subjected me, a fellow member of the One True Faith, to persecution. My father was an elder in the Meeting. I went home and reported Fern Hampton to him, and he violated the Quaker stand on nonviolence by giving me a paddling too.

I was surrounded by backsliders.

Now I am Fern Hampton's pastor and have forgiven her, though I'm still suspicious of her. Underneath her plain, gray dress lurks a woman longing to wear red and drive a Town Car. I take what she says with a grain of salt, knowing the compromises she's made. It's like Dale Hinshaw said back in 1974: "We'll have to keep an eye on that one. She could be trouble."

Now Fern Hampton is retired and devotes her considerable energies to the Friendly Women's Circle quilt project and Brother Norman's shoe ministry to the Choctaw Indians. But it might be a trick to lull us into complacency. Once you've dined at sin's table, it is a strong temptation to go back for seconds. So we're watching her closely.

School in our town begins the first Tuesday after Labor Day, which is the way it has always been and always will be, change being something we don't take to here. Which is why most of the kids who grow up in our town can't move away fast enough. Then they turn forty and are tired of progress and want to come back. They wake up one day and it occurs to them that the television remote control is smarter than them, and they find themselves pulled toward home, toward their own kind, where brilliance and progress are suspect.

I was walking my son Levi to school the day after Labor Day. It was his first day of first grade. He was carrying a cigar box with his school supplies: three pink erasers, six Laddie pencils—sharpened—eight crayons, one pair of safety scissors, two bottles of glue, and a ruler. He had his lunch money in his right pocket and his computer fee money in his left pocket.

The computer fee was a new development and not without controversy. The school board had deliberated for five years about whether to train kids to use the computer. The leading opponent of computers was Dale Hinshaw, who is the leading opponent of 'most everything new in Harmony. He'd read tabloid stories of kids hacking into the Pentagon computers and starting wars. He knew this for a fact because he'd read it.

He stood up at a school board meeting and said, "It happened with the Gulf War in 1990. That wasn't Saddam Hussein who started that war. That's just the government version. The real truth is that a kid in New Jersey triggered the whole thing on his computer. How you can even think of bringing computers in the schools is beyond me."

But it wasn't beyond the school board, who bought the computers anyway. Now Dale is thinking of running for the school board on a no-computer, no-progress platform. He believes the current school board is riddled with government informants whose plan is to create a One World Order starting with the Harmony schools.

I walked my son to the front door and into the school. Down the hall, past the principal's office to his classroom, which was right across from the gymnasium. I remembered playing dodgeball in the same gymnasium in the sixth grade on days it rained. I remember the football players throwing the ball so hard it imprinted my body on the wall. I remember them laughing. I was turning my son loose into this hard world.

I introduced Levi to his teacher, Mrs. Hester, who is Baptist and uses titles. Her name was written on the chalkboard: *Mrs. Hester.*

I shook her hand and said, "Hello, Mrs. Hester. This is my son Levi. He's in your class this year."

Mrs. Hester took him by the hand and showed him his desk. Second row on the left, third seat from the front.

This, then, was the moment of his growing up. I wanted to kiss him and rub his burry head. Wanted him to be two days old again and coming home from the hospital. He was scared. All the kids were. Sitting in their chairs, verging on tears.

I walked toward the door, then turned and looked back. He was watching me. His baby teeth were gone. My toothless son. He looked like Gabby Hayes sitting there. Like a little old man on his first day at the nursing home. Brave on the outside, wobbling on the inside.

"I'm fine. I'll be fine. You go on home. Don't worry, I'll be fine."

We learn that in first grade.

I stepped into the hallway and watched him, unobserved, through the window on the door. Watched him open his cigar box and line up his Laddie pencils in the pencil tray. Watched him fold his hands and place them on the desk. Instinct. We smell chalk dust and something inside us says, "Fold your hands and look forward." We just know to do it.

*M*y wife could scarcely bear the first tearing of this mother-child strand. She stayed home and cried. I did my grieving alone, in the fifth pew. I was thinking how this was it, this was the Going Away. Twelve years from now he'll leave for college. Then he'll sit across the kitchen table and talk about a job six states away. We'll move his things in a U-Haul. We'll talk on the phone every Sunday night. Begging him to come for a visit, without making it sound like begging. Giving him room. Trying not to let the hurt show when his plans don't include coming home.

"No, son, don't you worry about Christmas. Don't give it a thought. Your mother and I understand. We know you're busy. You know we'll be thinking of you. Let's shoot for next summer. Don't forget we love you."

Putting a brave face on things. We learn that in first grade.

I went to fetch him at two-thirty. Waited outside the school, on the sidewalk, in front of the buses. Saw him skipping out the building toward me. I rubbed his burry head, laid my hand on his shoulder and felt his skinny bones.

"Hey, little man, how was your first day of school?"

"Neat. But if you're bad, you get your name written on the chalk-board," he told me.

"Back when I was little, they used to give paddlings," I told him.

"Did you ever get paddled?" he asked.

"One time," I told him. "It was for my religion. Faith is not always an easy thing. Try to remember that."

My hand dangled at my side. He reached up to hold it. Automatic, without thinking. Hold Daddy's hand. I wondered when that would end, when the day would come that my hand would hang empty.

We were walking past the Coffee Cup. I asked him if he was thirsty. Of course. Always thirsty.

We sat in a booth and shared a Coke. A rare treat.

"Let's not tell your mother about the Coke," I suggested. "It can be our secret."

ne day I'll grow old and need a nursing home. My son will take me. He'll wheel me through the doors to my room. He'll take me by the hand and bend over my form and speak into my wizened ear, "Hey, Dad, remember when I was little and you'd walk me home from school and we'd stop at the Coffee Cup for a Coke?"

I'll squeeze his hand.

Oh, yes, I remember. I'll never forget. Never forget the day you were born. Never forget your burry head. Never forget you lining up your pencils and being brave. Never forget you folding your hands and looking forward. Never forget you taking my hand. Never forget hauling your things six states away.

He'll rise to leave. "I'll be back soon, Dad. I promise. Will you be all right?"

"I'm fine," I'll tell him. "I'll be fine. You go on home. Don't worry, I'll be fine."

Putting on a brave face.

We learn that in first grade.

f o u r t e e n

Noodle Day

s far back as I can remember, the Harmony Corn and
Sausage Days have been held the second week of September
on the town square. The week before, men from the
Optimist's Club hang the Corn and Sausage Days banner across Main
Street and the Chamber of Commerce selects the Sausage Queen, who
gets to ride down Main Street in Harvey Muldock's 1951 Plymouth
Cranbrook convertible, right behind the Shriners and just in front of the
Odd Fellows Lodge.

The highlight of Corn and Sausage Days is the Chicken Noodle
Dinner put on by the Friendly Women's Circle and held in the meetinghouse basement. Their motto is "Meeting All Your Noodle Needs
Since 1964." The Chicken Noodle Dinner is *the* event of the year for the
Circle and they take it seriously—and don't you forget it. If you are
elected to the presidency of the Friendly Women's Circle, you had better be able to pull off the Chicken Noodle Dinner or impeachment proceedings will commence.

I remember, as a child, going with my mother to the meetinghouse
every Tuesday morning while she and the Friendly Women made the

noodles. Their faces smudged with flour, wisps of hair hanging down. It was my job to cut the noodles. The ladies would roll the dough flat on the countertop, and I would run the noodle cutter over the dough. My mother would caution me to pay attention and cut straight. The ladies would divide the noodles and hang them on a noodle rack to dry overnight, then the next morning bag them up and store them in the freezer in the meetinghouse basement.

The freezer was bought in 1964, the first year the Friendly Women's Circle put on the Chicken Noodle Dinner. They cleared two hundred dollars and spent it on a Crosley Shelvador freezer, which is still lumbering along, down in the basement underneath the stairs. We can hear it on Sunday morning when we're waiting in the silence for the Lord to speak. We can hear the *tick, tick, tick* of the Regulator clock and the *hummm* of the Crosley freezer. We sit in the pews and think of those noodles and Corn and Sausage Days. Harvey Muldock thinks of his convertible. The teenage boys dream of the Sausage Queen. Then we go home at eleven-thirty, whether the Lord has spoken or not.

When I was growing up, we would walk from Sunday meeting down the sidewalk to my grandparents' home and eat fried chicken and green beans from their garden. Mashed potatoes and corn on the cob. Afterwards, if it was summer, we would sit on the front porch and make ice cream and visit, or maybe take a nap. Sometimes Harvey Muldock, who lived across the street, would swing open his garage doors, back his 1951 convertible out of the garage, and take us for rides in the country.

Now my grandparents are gone, and the torch has been passed to my parents. We were at my parents' house eating Sunday dinner when my mother mentioned how one of the cabinet doors in the meetinghouse kitchen had worked loose from the hinge and needed fixing. This was the week before the Chicken Noodle Dinner. My mother was in charge and wanted everything shipshape, right down to the cabinet doors. The ladies roll into the kitchen on Friday morning and do a shakedown cruise to check all the systems. By that time the Crosley is full with the year's effort. Chicken on one side, noodles on the other.

These are not ordinary chickens. These are Rhode Island Reds, straight from Asa Peacock's farm. Asa himself drove to the hatchery in early May and hand-fed those chickens all through the summer. He put a television set in the chicken coop, so the chickens would sit around and watch TV and get fat. Asa's wife, Jessie, dressed them out the first week of September before hauling them into town to store in the Crosley. She was putting the last of the chicken away when I went downstairs to fix the cabinet door.

"Hello, Sam," she said. "How's your mother?"

"Getting a little nervous," I told her. "She's been after me to fix this door."

I set my toolbox down and looked at the door. The wood had worn away from the screw. I'd have to drill new holes and reset the hinge. I lifted my drill from the box and looked around for a plug-in. It was an old kitchen; there weren't many outlets. The closest one was behind the freezer. I unplugged the freezer, plugged in the drill, bore new holes, and reset the hinge. As I was cleaning up, the phone rang. It was my mother, calling to see if I'd fixed the door.

"We're coming in this Friday. I want everything working," she told me.

I assured her everything was fine.

Then I carried my toolbox upstairs to my office and started working on my sermon. I had been preaching a sermon series on the Lord's Prayer, which had not gotten off to a good start. The first sermon was titled "Our Father...and Our Mother, Too." It was my effort to talk about God's feminine, nurturing side, which the professors at seminary had told me people wanted. But they had never met these people.

Now I was up to "Forgive us our trespasses as we forgive those who trespass against us." This was a sermon we needed. There are people in this town I don't like and don't know why, except that my father didn't like them and passed the dislike down to me, an unbroken chain of grudge and blame. Our ancestors had named this town Harmony in obedience to the apostle Paul, who encouraged the early Christians to "live in harmony with one another." I don't think our town was what he had in mind.

Walking home from the meetinghouse, I felt wonderfully good. Fixing the cabinet door, writing my sermon.

"This is real ministry," I thought to myself. "This is what God created me to do. This is my life's work."

That Friday morning I went to the meetinghouse early to bring a devotional to the Friendly Women's Circle. They were clustered in the kitchen, the freezer door was standing open. Pale pink chicken blood was dripping from the freezer shelves, running across the floor to the drain. There was a terrible odor. My mother was weeping.

My knees felt weak. I remembered unplugging the freezer to plug in my drill. Had I plugged the freezer back in? I couldn't remember. I felt sick.

I asked the ladies to step aside, to let me see behind the freezer. I stood on my tiptoes and peered at the plug-in. Oh, no. The freezer was unplugged, just as I had left it. I broke out in a prickly heat. This, then, was the end of my ministry, just as I was starting to enjoy it. What should I do?

I advised the ladies to stand back. I drew back my left hand and smacked the freezer hard, while plugging in the plug with my right hand. The freezer hummed to life.

"Must have been a short," I told them. "This freezer's getting old. Probably time to buy a new one."

The women were crying.

I said, "Don't be discouraged. We can make more noodles. I'll help you."

It took all day and into the evening. I cut the noodles, just like I did when I was a little boy. My mother cautioned me to pay attention and cut straight. We separated the noodles and hung them up to dry. Noodles everywhere, strung on clotheslines across the basement and draped across the pews upstairs.

Jessie Peacock went to the Kroger, bought thirty chickens, boiled them, and picked off the meat, grieving the whole time they weren't Rhode Island Reds.

We came back on Saturday morning. The noodles were dry. We cooked them tender and stirred in the chicken. The people began lining up at the doors. They streamed through for three solid hours. The women were everywhere—pouring tea, stirring noodles, cleaning dishes, and wiping tables. By two o'clock we had served the last dinner and at five o'clock the last dish was wiped dry and the floor was mopped.

It was all people talked about the next day at church. How everyone pitched in and worked hard to overcome a crisis. My mother stood and spoke of how all things work for good for them who love the Lord. Then Jessie Peacock told how I had worked harder than anyone, and how glad she was that I was their pastor and what an example of faith I was. She had forgotten all about the chickens.

I didn't say anything. I had come to church prepared to confess. I was going to tell them I had left the freezer unplugged, but sitting there, listening to them, I decided not to. The Lord moves in mysterious ways. This had been a good thing. It had caused them to work together. It had restored their faith and renewed their confidence. Who was I to cheapen that? So I kept quiet. For their sake.

*T*he next day I drove to Sears in the city and bought the Friendly Women's Circle a new freezer. I bought myself a cordless drill. That Tuesday, two men delivered the new freezer, humping it down the stairs. They hauled the Crosley to the dump. The women stood around the new freezer, patting it, smiling and proud.

My mother grinned and clapped her hands. "Come on, Friendly Women, let's make those noodles."

I'll tell them someday, but not anytime soon. Maybe when I've been here twenty-five years.

I went up to my office and began working on my new sermon, "Lead Us Not into Temptation, but Deliver Us from All Evil."

I bowed my head to pray. "Yes, Lord, teach us this lesson. For sometimes we are too tricky for our own good. Help us to depend on You and not upon our cleverness. And Lord, if those women should ever learn the truth, protect and guard Your humble servant. Amen."

fifteen

The World

I was in first grade when I learned that religious faith would not be easy to sustain. I bowed my head to pray at lunch, just as my parents had taught me.

> *Thank You, God, for our food,*
> *for homes and health and all things good.*
> *For the wind and the rain and the sun above,*
> *And most of all for those we love.*

Then I said "Amen" and raised my head just as Jerry Porter hit me on the arm and called me a twinkie. This wasn't like home, where I was patted on the head and given an extra helping of macaroni and cheese. This was The World. This was what Pastor Taylor cautioned us about every Sunday morning at Harmony Friends Meeting.

"The World will persecute you for your faith. Jesus didn't have it easy. Neither will you. Don't you forget it. There's hard times ahead. Be strong."

The next Sunday at church, I told my Sunday school teacher, Bea

Majors, about Jerry Porter hitting me for praying. She told me it was the price of faith. If I had been a student of the Scriptures, I would have pointed out the biblical injunction against public prayer. Matthew 6:6. Printed in red ink, straight from the Lord's own mouth. "But when you pray, go into your room and shut the door and pray…" It would have saved me a lot of bruises.

Even though it was a dangerous half hour, I enjoyed school lunch most of all. I liked the order of it. Lining up in the classroom in front of the fish tank, marching down the hallway to the cafeteria, reaching down in the milk cooler and pulling out a chocolate milk. Sitting at a long table and talking until Mr. Michaels, the principal, put a classical music album on the record player which was the signal to stop talking and start eating. To this day, whenever I hear Beethoven, I think of Salisbury steak, mashed potatoes, and diced peaches.

I especially liked the food trays. At our house, all the food ran together on our plates. The green bean juice got mixed in with the applesauce, which spilled over on the corn. I didn't care for that and wouldn't eat it. My mother told me to clean my plate, that kids in Africa didn't have any food. I offered to send them my supper.

What I liked about the school food was that it knew its place. There was the meat section of the tray. It was the biggest section of all, in the lower right-hand corner. Next to it was the vegetable section, which was a circle in the lower left corner. On the left edge of the tray was where you laid the silverware, along with your napkin and drinking straw. The fruit went in the upper left corner, and next to it, in the top center section, was the dessert. In the upper right corner was where you set your cardboard container of milk. Chocolate milk if you were a boy, white milk if you were a girl.

The trays were a disservice, leading us to believe the rest of life would be orderly, though it never was. They'd have been better off stirring our food together and telling us that was how the world was—

mixed up and out of kilter. Instead, they had us walk in lines and didn't let our food run together. They taught us harmony and sent us forth into chaos.

I had forgotten all about the trays until I went to eat lunch with my son, Levi, the second week of school. I signed in at the office and walked down the hallway toward his classroom. I passed the sixth-grade hallway and heard Miss Fishbeck calling out words for a spelling bee. I listened as Amanda Hodge spelled the word *methodical. M-e-t-h-o-d-i-c-a-l.* The talk at the Coffee Cup was that she might win the county spelling bee.

My son's class was lined up in the hallway. Mrs. Hester marched us to the cafeteria where the ladies spooned out our food in sections. We sat at a long table. It reminded me of a prison table, where the convicts ate and planned their escapes. I was sandwiched between Levi and a little boy named Adam Fleming.

My son had told me about Adam—how Adam's name was written on the chalkboard at least once a day, how he'd been sent to the principal's office two times already, how none of the kids liked him.

"He's a liar," my son reported. "And once at recess he kicked Billy Grant right in the stomach. On purpose. If he messes with me, I'll karate chop him."

The Flemings lived east of town in a trailer. Adam and his two little sisters and his parents had moved to town the year before. Adam's daddy, Wayne, worked nights at the Kroger waxing the floors, and his mother labored at the McDonald's down near the interstate.

Then early one morning Wayne Fleming came home from work to find the kids asleep and his wife gone. There was a note on the table which read, *Don't try to find me. I've gone away.*

The rumor was that she'd met a trucker and had gone west with him. Our thoughts toward her were not charitable. The women from the meeting had been taking food out to the trailer and the lady who worked at the Kroger deli let Wayne take home the day-old bread and the chicken wings that didn't sell. The nights were hardest, when Wayne would tuck the children into bed and they would cry for their mommy. People said they were better off, but it didn't feel that way to Adam and his sisters.

Their daddy never knew what to tell them, so he never said anything. He would just hold them until they fell asleep. Then he'd tidy up the trailer and start the laundry and wash the dishes. Then the retired neighbor lady would come sleep on the couch, and Wayne would leave for the Kroger.

I knew about all this as I was kind of their pastor, since they'd come to our meeting the Easter before. I'd gone to visit them a time or two and had seen Wayne at Kroger, when I'd go there late at night for ice cream. We took to visiting in the aisles and struck up a kind of friendship. When his wife ran off with the trucker, Wayne called to tell me.

I mentioned their need to the Friendly Women's Circle who were casting about for a new project. They decided to take on the Flemings. But as magnificent as those women were, they were no replacement for a mother. Adam and his sisters still cried themselves to sleep.

I had told my son that Adam didn't have the blessings he had and to treat him nice.

Now Adam was sitting next to Levi and me in the school cafeteria. He said, "My daddy sleeps in the daytime. He doesn't eat lunch."

I said, "Hey, Adam, why don't I come next week and have lunch with you. Would you like that?"

He said he would. Then he said, "My mommy came to eat lunch

with me yesterday. Have you met my mommy? She's a good mommy. She's real nice."

Hoping if he said it enough times, it'd make it true.

I said, "I don't know your mother well, but I bet she's nice."

He said, "She's real nice. When I get home from school she has cookies for me. And she buys me lots of toys. Anything I want."

A little girl across the table shrieked, "He's lying. He's a liar. His mommy's gone. She ran off."

"Shut your face," Adam screamed and lunged at her. I grabbed hold of him and pulled him back. He was shaking with rage. Then he leaned into me and began to cry.

The lunchroom monitor marched over, frowning, and told Adam if he didn't settle down, he'd have to sit off by himself at the quiet table.

This is The World's response to suffering. We want it out of sight, off by itself over at the quiet table.

Raw pain alarms us. It reminds us that life isn't as orderly as we'd hoped. We demand that pain settle down before we shuffle it off to the quiet table. We want pain to stay in its own little section, want to keep it from spilling over into the other parts of life. Just like those lunch trays. Keep pain in its own little compartment.

I held Adam to me, thinking of his mother. Wondering if her joy in running off was worth all this. I thought of Wayne having to teach his children they were still worth loving and worth having. What a large task, when all the evidence seems otherwise.

This was The World Pastor Taylor had warned against. A world where some parents cared more about their happiness than they did their children. I thought of the cold evil committed by folks looking to be happy.

The World.

I held that little boy to me and thought hopeful thoughts of a New World. Yearning for it as never before. A New World.

A world where God has set up housekeeping, where God will live right with us, and we with Him. He'll wipe the tears from our eyes, and death will die. No more crying, no more sorrow, no more pain, no more.

I held that crying boy to me and thought my hopeful thoughts.

Sixteen

Mutiny

The Quaker religion began in 1647 and was based on the premise that God could be known directly by all persons. Quakers believed you didn't need a priest to approach God on your behalf, that you could approach God yourself. A kind of do-it-yourself religion. It was a radical concept at the time and was strongly opposed, mostly by priests who had made a handsome living approaching God on other people's behalf.

The Quaker fondness for self-sufficiency continues to this day—we would never think of hiring a plumber or electrician to work in the meetinghouse. Consequently, our meetinghouse toilet gets stopped up a lot, and when the furnace kicks on, the freezer in the basement blows a fuse. Any suggestion to hire a professional to fix these problems is met with derision by staunch Quakers accustomed to standing on their own two feet.

Not hiring professionals has become a test of one's faith. Three hundred years ago, the Quaker proverbs included "There is that of God in every person" and "Thou shalt not kill." Today, it is "We can fix that toilet ourselves" and "If we all pitched in, we could paint the meetinghouse together."

Except we never get around to fixing anything, because when it gets mentioned during our church's monthly business meeting that we need to paint the meetinghouse, Dale Hinshaw scoffs and says, "Well, I'll tell you one thing right now. Ever since they took lead out of paint, it hasn't been worth a darn. Used to be a paint job would last twenty, maybe thirty years, but not anymore. Why don't we have Sam drive up to Canada and buy some paint with lead in it, so it'll last."

I sit quietly, thinking to myself: This is why I went to seminary—so I could drive to Canada and buy lead paint.

The young mothers sit there, horrified, envisioning their children licking lead paint and suffering brain damage.

One of them raises her hand, timidly. "Isn't lead kind of dangerous?" she asks.

"Naw," Dale scoffs, "that's a government lie. The paint companies bribed Congress to take lead out so we'd have to paint our houses more often and buy more paint. It's a big racket. Lead never hurt nobody."

This is Dale Hinshaw at his finest, dismissing a whole body of scientific research in one fell swoop.

The mothers sit there, blinking and dazed. This is not what they'd heard about Quakers. They'd read about the Quakers' opposition to war and slavery, about our beliefs in simplicity, reconciliation, and integrity. They come to church expecting enlightenment and meet Dale Hinshaw instead.

This is why our church never grows. Just when we've gotten someone committed enough to come to our monthly business meeting, Dale Hinshaw is honing his latest conspiracy theory. It makes the new people leery about sticking around; they worry they're joining some kind of weird cult.

*I*t happened again in October, when the toilet in the women's bathroom broke and needed replacing. Uly Grant offered to donate a brand-new toilet from the Grant Hardware Emporium.

In a fit of new convert enthusiasm, he even offered to install it.

Dale Hinshaw rose to his feet. "Well, Uly, you do what you want, but I think there's a higher principle involved here, something many of you probably haven't thought about, and that is the topic of these new low-flow toilets. They don't work. You got to flush 'em two or three times. Why don't I drive up to the city to a secondhand store and see if I can get us a used one."

The women began to murmur, ruminating about used toilets. Dale would buy the cheapest one, probably one from the men's room of an old gas station. It would be dark brown with rust. It would have cigarette burns on the toilet seat. The women grimaced.

Dale continued, "I tell you, the government's gone too far this time, telling us what kind of toilets we can put in our own homes. That ain't right."

Miriam Hodge spoke up, the picture of Quaker reasonableness. "Aren't the new toilets supposed to use less water, so we can better preserve our limited natural resources?"

Dale said, "Miriam, this ain't about water. This is about liberty. This is about freedom. They're starting with our toilets, then it'll be our guns, then it'll be the vote. You watch and see. No, I can't agree with this at all. It's time we took a stand."

Suddenly the installation of a toilet had become a political issue, a test of our patriotism, a challenge to the Bill of Rights.

The trouble with belonging to a religion founded on rebellion is that the spirit of rebellion is never exhausted. It just finds different things to rebel against. First we rebelled against empty religious practices, then against war and slavery. Now we had toilets squarely in our sights.

After the meeting was over, the women gathered in a corner, talking, their voices raised. I was standing with Uly. The women headed toward us. Fern Hampton emerged from their ranks.

"If we don't get a new toilet by next Sunday, the women of this meeting are going on strike," Fern declared. "No more pitch-in dinners. No more teaching Sunday school classes. No more serving on committees. No more noodles. You think about that."

Then, having fired their shot across our bow, they turned and marched away.

Mutiny. This was getting ugly. No more noodles.

I turned to Uly. "What are we gonna do?" I asked him.

He said, "Meet me at the back door of the meetinghouse tonight at ten o'clock. Don't tell a soul. Come alone. Bring your flashlight. Wear dark clothes."

I wondered all day what Uly had in store. Barbara and I went to bed at nine-thirty. She fell asleep. At nine-fifty I slipped out of bed, pulled on my dark clothes, and grabbed my flashlight. I walked the four blocks to the meetinghouse and stood at the back door, in the shadows.

A pickup truck, its headlights off, coasted into the meetinghouse parking lot and pulled up next to the back door. The driver's door eased open, and Uly slid out of the truck, noiselessly.

He motioned me to the back of the truck. There was a brand-new, low-flow toilet perched in the truck bed.

"Uly, it's beautiful," I told him.

"Shh!" Uly whispered. "Help me lift it out." We snuck the toilet into the meetinghouse and down the stairs to the women's bathroom.

Uly said, "Turn on your flashlight."

I flipped it on. It looked odd in there, with the subtle mingling of shadow and light. It felt wrong to be there, a violation of everything I'd been taught. Spurning the bright light of truth and hiding in the shadows. I felt guilty. I recalled Pastor Taylor admonishing us "to present ourselves to God as one approved, a workman who has no need to be ashamed…" Now here I was, slinking around in the shadows of the women's restroom.

Uly said, "You hold the flashlight; I'll put in the new toilet."

It was just about that time that Mr. and Mrs. Dale Hinshaw were driving past on their way home from her sister's house in the city. Dale and his wife had bought a cellular phone the week before and Dale wanted to drive to the city so he could phone someone from the car to tell them he was calling from the car. Halfway to the city, they phoned her sister to say they were on their way.

"Where you calling from?" she asked Dale.

"We're about forty miles out and heading your way," Dale replied. "We just passed the Little Point exit."

She said, "You sound funny."

He said, "I'm calling from the car." He said it casually, like it was no big deal.

"Dale's calling from the car," she yelled to her husband, amazed.

Dale showed them the cell phone when they arrived. They passed the phone around and marveled at it. Then Dale told them about the toilet controversy and how he'd had to stand firm against low-flow toilets.

"You have to flush 'em two or three times," he complained.

They nodded their heads in firm agreement.

Now Dale and the missus were on their way home. They were driving past the meetinghouse when Dale noticed a flash of light coming from the window of the women's bathroom.

He pulled to a stop. There it was again. Yes, a light. Someone was in there. Dale eased around the corner and into the church parking lot. A pickup truck was pulled up to the back door.

"Burglars!" he cried out. "Probably from the city."

Every bad thing that happened in our town was blamed on people from the city. Now Dale had caught them in the act. What a glorious day this had been! First, getting to stand firm for truth, then using his cellular phone. Now he had caught some burglars. He pulled out his cellular phone and dialed 911, the first time he'd ever done that. His hand was shaking; he could barely punch in the numbers.

A lady answered the phone.

"This is Dale Hinshaw. I'm calling from my cellular phone. I'm outside the Harmony Friends meetinghouse. There's a pack of burglars from the city in there, right now, robbing us blind."

Ten minutes later the Harmony police car pulled alongside Dale. It was Bernie Rogers.

Dale climbed out of his car. He said, "Bernie, I'm the one who called. Right here from my cell phone."

He showed Bernie his cell phone.

Dale continued, "It looks like we got some burglars in the meetinghouse. Why don't you go in and chase them out?"

Dale paused and looked at Bernie's considerable paunch.

"Anyway, chase 'em out as best you can. I'll wait for them in the bushes. When they run out, I'll knock 'em on the head with that stick of yours. Why don't you give that to me?"

Bernie handed Dale his nightstick.

Bernie and Dale crept to the back door. It was unlocked. Dale hid in the bushes. Bernie opened the door, lumbered down the stairs, and paused outside the women's restroom. He heard voices.

Bernie thought one of the voices sounded like mine. What would the pastor be doing in the women's bathroom in the middle of the night? It couldn't be good.

He called out, "Sam, is that you in there?"

Uly and I froze. We were treed.

I turned on the light and opened the door. There was Bernie, his hand resting on his pistol.

Bernie looked in at me and Uly. He said, "What you doing in here, boys?" He seemed almost afraid to ask.

Putting in a new toilet, we told him.

"In the middle of the night?" he asked. "Using a flashlight and wearing dark clothes?"

I told him about Dale Hinshaw not wanting a new toilet and the women not making any more noodles.

"No more noodles," Bernie said, alarmed at the prospect.

"Not a one," I told him. Then I asked Bernie why he was there.

He said, "Dale Hinshaw called us on his cell phone. He thinks you're burglars from the city. He's waiting outside to knock you on the head with a stick. Don't go out the back door."

I pleaded with Bernie, "Don't tell Dale we're in here. Go tell him there was no one here, and send him home." I promised him a free noodle dinner at our annual Chicken Noodle Dinner.

"It's a deal," Bernie said. We shook on it. Then he left and so did Dale. We heard them driving away. Uly and I finished putting in the new toilet, then went home and went to bed.

I saw Dale Hinshaw the next morning at the Coffee Cup. He said, "Well, you missed all the excitement last night. There were burglars at the meetinghouse. Me and Bernie, we tried to catch them, but they had guns so we let 'em go. They ran out the front door and got away. We got a look at them though. They were from the city."

"Oh, my," I said. "It's a good thing you were there to help Bernie."

"I called him on my cell phone," Dale said. He pulled the phone from his pocket and laid it on the counter. "Aren't these something?" he marveled.

"Yeah, but I read somewhere they give you cancer," I told him.

He said, "No. Really?"

I said, "Yeah, it turns out the phone companies bribed Congress not to say anything about it, so they could sell more phones and make more money. It's all a racket."

Dale said, "Well, I'll be."

"Yep, that's what I heard," I told him.

He began to rub his ear and look anxious.

That was on a Monday. The next Sunday, Fern Hampton rose up from the sixth row during our prayer time and announced what a joy it was to have a new low-flow toilet in the women's restroom. She invited the ladies to come see it after worship, then invited them to make noodles on Tuesday morning. All the men smiled, except for Dale.

I expected him to be angry. Instead, he raised his hand and asked for prayer.

"I think I might have cancer of the ear," he said. "Think I got it from my cell phone. I'm going to the doctor this week. Can you pray for me?"

Dale's wife sat beside him, twisting her hands and looking anguished.

I felt terrible.

In 1647, we Quakers, with high and holy hopes, launched an experiment in holy living, dedicated to the ideals of simplicity, reconciliation, and integrity. But after a while we forsook integrity and became mired in deceit. It is all the sadder because of our heritage. We come from a people whose word was their bond, and we profaned their memory with our indifference to truth. I was the worst of all.

I went to Dale after worship and confessed to lying about cell phones causing cancer. He sagged with relief.

"Well," Dale said, "as long as we're confessing, I think maybe I stretched it a little bit about low-flow toilets. Most of the time it only takes one flush."

We shook hands, reconciled with truth and one another.

No more trickery, I told myself. No more slinking around in the shadows. I'm going to present myself to God as one approved, a workman who has no need to be ashamed. I have a heritage, after all, a legacy to live up to. A straightforward past, with high and holy hopes of a forthright future.

Seventeen

The Twins

Paul and Judy Iverson came to Harmony Friends Meeting the first week of September. It wasn't unusual for our church to have visitors. What was odd about Paul and Judy Iverson was that they came back a second time.

Most people attend our church out of obligation, knowing if they miss a Sunday they'll feel guilty because we'll call them on the phone and contribute to that feeling. If you don't come to church, you'd better have a good reason. Staying home to read the Sunday paper is not acceptable. Visiting your mother is a good reason. Going on vacation is a valid excuse, but one you shouldn't overuse. Staying home from church because you're sick is permissible, though you need to be pretty sick. Smallpox or polio or something such as that.

Then Paul and Judy Iverson moved here from the city and attended meeting for worship on their very first Sunday and stunned us by returning a second time. We were so surprised that Dale Hinshaw called a meeting of the elders to talk about what we should do, and how we could trick them into staying.

Dale proposed putting them on a committee as soon as possible so they'd feel bound to stay.

"Let's give 'em a job so they can't escape," he said.

Miriam Hodge had talked with the Iversons both times they were here. She told us everything she knew about them. They had been married eleven years. Paul was a sixth-grade school teacher. Miss Fishbeck was retiring at the end of the school year, and Paul Iverson was to be her replacement. They'd bought an old house and moved here early to fix it up.

"We'll need a church nursery," Miriam said. "They're adopting a baby. All the way from China."

That pretty well silenced us. It took a while to digest that. A Chinese baby. In Harmony.

*P*aul and Judy had tried since they were married to have children, but couldn't. Then one day they watched a television show about baby girls in China left in the streets to die. It was more than they could bear. The very next week Judy read a story in a magazine about a couple who had gone to China to adopt a baby girl. There was a phone number at the end of the article, which you could call for information. They called.

Now it was a year later, and they were three weeks away from going to China to get their baby girl. They'd told Miriam all about it, about having to fly to Los Angeles, then to Hong Kong, then to Beijing, then take an overnight train to get their baby girl.

So the church needed a nursery, and soon. We didn't have one. When our meetinghouse had been built in 1826, nurseries were not a high priority. Back in those days, children suffered through worship right alongside their parents.

Miriam said, "You know, there's that storage closet just inside the door. I think that would hold a couple cribs and a rocker. We could fix it up nice."

So that's what we did. Miriam Hodge sewed new curtains. Dale Hinshaw painted the walls yellow, and his wife hung Panda bear wallpaper so the little girl would feel at home. The Friendly Women's Circle paid for new carpet. It was beautiful. It was ready for a little Chinese baby.

We dedicated the nursery the Sunday before Paul and Judy left for China. We had a prayer and sang "Jesus Loves the Little Children." I quoted from Mark 10:14, where Jesus told us to suffer the little children. Suffer, I thought, was precisely the right word. Paul thanked us and Judy cried. Then we ate cake and drank red punch, but not on the new carpet.

A baby! Just think of it. A baby in the meeting. In our very own nursery. A little girl with a good tan and dark hair. In our nursery.

They left that Tuesday. Traveled for three days. On Friday, the phone rang in the meetinghouse office. Frank the secretary answered. It was Paul and Judy. There was a lot of static and he could hardly hear them.

Then the static stopped, just for a moment, and he heard Judy say "twins." Twins! Then he heard the word "Siamese." At least that's what it sounded like. Siamese twins. Then the phone went dead and that was it.

Frank sat at his desk, stunned. Siamese twins. Paul and Judy Iverson had adopted Siamese twins. Oh, my.

Frank didn't know what to think. He walked into the nursery and looked at the crib. It was an old crib, but Mrs. Dale Hinshaw had painted it and we'd bought a new mattress for it.

"It won't be big enough," Frank thought. "Not for Siamese twins." He'd seen pictures of Siamese twins. They'd need a bigger crib. Those poor kids. Poor Paul and Judy. Such brave people to adopt these children, to give them a chance at life. What fine people.

Maybe he should tell someone. He wasn't sure. Maybe he should call

Bob Miles Jr. at the *Herald* and get a fund drive going. Maybe set out a change jar at the Coffee Cup. Then he decided against it. No use in making a spectacle of this, he thought. No sense in getting people all worked up. Folks will find out soon enough. He marveled again at Paul and Judy. Such brave, kind people.

Frank knew then what he'd do. He'd build a new crib. A big crib. A crib for the Iverson Siamese twins.

*H*e stayed up that night, drawing the plans. His idea was a simple one—he'd buy two matching cribs, remove one side from each crib, and fasten the cribs together. Yes, that would work. It would be expensive, but it would be worth it. He'd pay for it himself. He didn't have much money, but he had enough. He'd been saving to buy a new lawn mower, but this was more important.

It took him a week to build it. The Iversons were due at church the next Sunday. On Saturday, he took the cribs apart and hauled them to the meetinghouse. It was hot, hard work. He carried them down the sidewalk and up the stairs into the meetinghouse.

It took two hours to put the cribs together. They filled the nursery. Frank checked for rough edges and splinters. He didn't want the babies to hurt themselves. Those poor children would have enough to overcome. He ran his finger over the finish. It was smooth as a Siamese baby's bottom.

He stretched the new sheets on the mattresses. It brought back memories of his little girl. Forty years ago. Making her little bed. Now she was grown and four states away. His two granddaughters were with her. He saw them once a year at Christmas. He barely knew them. He tried not to think about it.

Then he thought of those little Siamese twins. Those sweet little girls. He would help take care of them. He'd helped care for children once before. They'd need extra help, extra love. He could do it. He was sure of it. Everything would be fine. Maybe this was why God had brought him to Harmony Friends. To help the Iversons.

Then another thought came to mind. What would they wear? He worried about that. Judy would be too busy to sew. Paul would be teaching school.

Frank thought, I'll learn to sew. I can do that. It can't be that hard.

He remembered back to his mother sewing on a Singer treadle. Pumping up and down, feeding the material past the needle. He could do that. He'd make them dresses. He'd buy them shoes. Oh, he hadn't even thought of that. How many shoes would they need? Two? Three? Four? He wasn't sure.

*H*e stood back from the crib and looked at it. It was lovely. It was big, but it was beautiful. Painted white with little ducky sheets. The twins deserved it. He was so proud.

Then Frank returned home and went down to the basement, to his wife's sewing room. It was the first time he'd been in it since her death. It was just as she'd left it. It even smelled like her. He looked at her sewing machine. It wasn't anything like his mother's. He couldn't find the switch to turn it on. He called Fern Hampton of the Friendly Women's Circle.

"Can you sew?" he asked her.

"Of course," she answered, "Why do you want to know?"

"I can't say," Frank told her. "Just be ready."

The next day was Sunday. He woke up early. He wore his best suit and got to the meetinghouse an hour before church. He dusted the crib and refolded the blankets. He wiped down the changing table.

Diapers! Oh my, what would those Siamese twins do for diapers? Diapers could be a problem.

Get a grip on yourself, Frank told himself. You can't worry about these things. Everything will be fine. Trust the Lord.

People began to arrive for worship. They gathered in the front hall-way, waiting for the Iversons.

Frank hoped everyone would be polite, would not stare or gasp. Then he thought, These are good people. They'll come through.

He heard someone yell, "Here they come!" and the front doors opened, and there stood Paul and Judy holding their Chinese twins. Paul held one and Judy held the other. Chinese twins!

People were shocked. Twins! They couldn't believe it. Beautiful, precious Chinese twins. People were shocked.

Judy asked, "Didn't Frank tell you? We called to tell you we had twins."

Everyone turned and looked at Frank.

You don't live seventy years without being quick on your feet. Frank said, "I've been too busy to tell anyone. I've made them a crib. Come see."

They filed into the nursery. A handful of people squeezed in around the crib. The rest of the Quakers peered in from the doorway, observing.

"Oh, Frank, it's beautiful," Judy said. They laid the Chinese twins on the ducky sheets. Two little girls with good tans and dark hair. Frank had never seen such black hair.

*f*rank stayed with the twins in the nursery while everyone else worshiped in the meeting room. Miriam Hodge helped him. He'd hold one, then the other. He changed their diapers. It all came back. Two wipes, three swipes, a fresh diaper, then a kiss on the head and you're done. Like riding a bicycle, you never forget.

Finally, he held them both. Rocking in the chair. Back and forth. Back and forth. One of the girls took his finger, then the other one did the same. They began sucking, their little gums nubbing on his fingers. He'd forgotten that feeling.

He thought of his two little granddaughters. He hadn't seen them since the funeral. Wouldn't see them until Christmas. At least he hoped he'd see them then. His daughter had phoned the week before and told him not to get his hopes up, that the girls were in ballet and had to practice every day. Plus, they were taking French lessons.

He wondered at that. French lessons? Why in the world did kids living in North Carolina need to speak French?

"French lessons!" he'd said to his daughter. "What good will that do? Whenever France gets in trouble, we have to go over there and bail 'em out. What makes French so special?"

Paul and Judy and the twins lived around the corner from Frank. Frank took to stopping by every day, on his way home from the meetinghouse. He'd sit with the kids while Paul worked on the house and Judy took a nap.

One afternoon, when Judy was at the store, Frank was holding the twins and thinking about Thanksgiving. It was a week away. Paul and Judy didn't have any family nearby. They were alone, just like Frank. This would be the first Thanksgiving since his wife had died. Maybe Paul and Judy and the twins could come to his house.

He asked Judy about it when she got home from the store.

"Say," Frank said, "I've just been thinking that if you don't have any plans, maybe you and Paul and the girls could come to my house for Thanksgiving." He held his breath. Oh Lord, please let her say yes. He didn't want to be alone.

"That would be nice," Judy said. "We'd love to. Thank you for asking."

So that Tuesday, Frank went to the Kroger and bought a turkey. A twenty pounder. Three cans of cranberry sauce. Two dozen rolls and instant mashed potatoes with a jar of gravy. Plus a twelve pack of RC Cola.

He woke up early Thanksgiving morning. Took the turkey from the refrigerator and squinted at the directions over his glasses. Why did they have to print these instructions so small? He saw the number *185*. There, that was it. One hundred and eighty-five degrees. He set the oven on bake at a hundred and eighty-five degrees. Bake for seven hours, the label read.

Frank put the turkey in the oven. This was a breeze. At one o'clock, he pulled the turkey from the oven. Opened the cans of cranberry sauce and poured them in a bowl. Stirred up the potatoes. Warmed up the gravy. At two o'clock, his doorbell rang.

They were here. Those nice people with their beautiful little girls. Frank hurried to the door and swung it open.

"Come in, come in," he said. "The turkey's done cooking. I just have to set the table."

Judy helped him. They set the turkey in the center. This was the best part. Cutting the turkey. Frank's favorite part.

But first, a prayer. Short and sweet. Cut to the chase. The Lord knows your heart and is not impressed with flowery speech. This is Frank's theory.

"Dear Lord, thank You for this food. Thank You for these babies. Please be with our families. Amen."

He cut into the turkey. It was a little pinker than he remembered turkey being. He cut down through the turkey. Pinker still. He kept cutting. There was a piece of plastic. Plastic? What was plastic doing in his turkey?

Judy asked, "Frank, did you take out the bag of giblets?"

"Giblets? What are giblets?" Frank asked.

Judy kind of grinned.

Well, you don't live seventy years without being quick on your feet.

Frank said, "You know, I believe the McDonald's over by the inter-state is open. How do you feel about Big Macs?"

"I like Big Macs," Judy said.

"So do I," said Paul.

So that's what they did. Judy cleared the table while Paul drove to McDonald's. Frank sat in his rocking chair, holding the girls, their little gums nubbing on his fingers.

The Iversons stayed four hours. The girls slept on Frank's bed with pillows piled around them, while Frank and Paul and Judy played Scrabble and drank RC Cola at the kitchen table. Every now and then, they'd sneak into Frank's bedroom and look in on the twins.

"Chinese twins. Isn't that something?" Frank said.

Then it was time for them to leave. Paul shook his hand and Judy kissed him on the cheek. The babies nubbed his finger.

I stopped by later that evening. I had been thinking of Frank the whole day, wondering how he was getting along.

He said, "It's been a good day, Sam. Paul and Judy were here. Got to hold my girls. It's been a good day. Lot to be thankful for."

I told him, "I sure hope the Iversons stick with us. I hope they don't leave the church. Hope they don't go to that new church out by the interstate. You know, the one that shows music on the screen and has a children's minister."

Frank said, "They're not looking for a children's minister. They're looking for love. I think they'll stick."

Then he looked at me and asked, "Sam, what are giblets?"

"I'm not certain," I said. "But I think you drink wine from 'em."

"I had wine once," Frank said. "On our wedding day. I didn't much care for it."

"Your wedding day?" I asked.

"No, the wine," Frank said.

Then he said, "I think I'm going to make it, Sam. When the missus died, I didn't think so…"

He choked a little as he spoke.

"But now I think I'm gonna make it."

He rocked back and forth. It was quiet in that room. Peaceful.

He held up his index finger and inspected it and chuckled. "You oughta see those little girls just chew on that finger. They really work it over."

"They'll do that."

Then Frank said, "You know, Thanksgiving isn't as easy as it looks."

"Nothing ever is," I told him. "Nothing ever is."

"I guess that's why the Lord gives us friends," he said.

"That is precisely the truth," I told him. "That is precisely the truth."

Eighteen

Roger and Tiffany

On the Saturday after Thanksgiving, our family went to the city to be with my brother Roger and his girlfriend, Tiffany. They had invited us for Thanksgiving dinner back in September. We spent the next two months trying to think of an excuse not to go, but couldn't come up with one. We are unimaginative people and thus are poor liars. Plus, we don't want to hurt anyone's feelings, so we end up doing a lot of things we don't want to do—like going to Tupperware parties and driving two hours to eat Thanksgiving dinner at an apartment in the city.

My mother was opposed to it. It didn't feel right to her—eating a Thanksgiving meal at someone else's home. To have someone else cook your family's Thanksgiving dinner seemed to her a moral failure, a lapse of duty. She'd never met Tiffany—none of us had—but my mother phoned Tiffany's apartment anyway and offered to bring the turkey.

Tiffany said, "Oh no, that's okay. Like, we're not really having turkey. Roger and I don't eat meat. We're vegans."

This startled my mother. Vegans? What in the world were vegans? She thought it was a new religion, that Roger had moved from

Harmony and joined a cult. How could that be? She had raised Roger in the church, had taught him in Sunday school, then he went to the city and met this Tiffany and joined a cult. What was he thinking?

Suddenly, she wanted to go to the city. She wanted to get Roger alone, away from Tiffany, and remind him of the goodness of the Lord.

She talked about it on our way to the city. We were riding together in my parents' Buick. My mother clutched her Bible, girding her loins for battle.

"They don't eat meat," she moaned. "Plus, they've joined a cult. The vegans."

"For crying out loud," my father said. "No meat! What are we going to eat? We shoulda just stayed home."

My mother said from the backseat, "Sam, I want you to talk with your brother about the Lord. You set him right."

I told her, "Mom, vegans are people who don't eat or wear anything having to do with animals. It's not a cult. Roger still believes in God. He just doesn't eat meat."

"For crying out loud," my father said.

"It was that college," my mother lamented. "We never should have sent him there."

*R*oger had graduated from Earlham College in Indiana. The college had been founded in 1847 by solemn Quakers who sent their children there to protect them from the stain of The World. But by the time Roger attended, there were seminars on Woodstock, and the professors wore sandals. An ominous sign. But my mother and father had sent him there anyway on the advice of Pastor Taylor, who was now dead and beyond accountability. Now they were reaping the bitter harvest—a no-meat Thanksgiving at an apartment in the city.

During college, Roger worked weekends at a bookstore, where he was exposed to seditious literature. He read about world religions and feminist theology and men who spent their weekends beating drums in the woods. Then he began to read poetry, which pleased my mother, who loved poetry. She particularly enjoyed Helen Steiner Rice.

When Roger told her he belonged to a poetry group, she was thrilled. He confided that he had even written a poem and wanted to know if she would like to hear it.

"Oh yes," she told him. "Please. Your very own poem! Think of that. How wonderful! Maybe I can use it for a devotional at our next Friendly Women's Circle."

She called my father into the kitchen and told him to sit down, that Roger had written a poem and was going to read it to them.

It was a poem about the exploitation of workers and the hypocrisy of capitalism. It ended with the torturous death of bankers, the rise of the working class, and country clubs being converted into housing for the homeless. Roger read his poem with great passion.

When he had finished reading, there was silence. Then my father said "For crying out loud," and got up and left the room.

When Roger went back to college, my mother tucked a treasury of Helen Steiner Rice poems in his backpack. Real poetry, where the words rhymed.

Roger had met Tiffany at a poetry reading. She had gone to college to major in education but had become disenchanted with traditional education's emphasis on hierarchy and had switched her major to sociology. By then, Roger had decided to study philosophy.

"For crying out loud," my father had said.

We pulled into the apartment complex where Tiffany lived. Climbed out of the Buick and went inside, up the stairs to the fourth floor. My mother gripped her Bible in her hand. My father was wheezing.

There was a sign on the door. I peered at it. It was from Thoreau, the first hippie. It read,

If a man does not keep pace with his companions, perhaps it is because he hears a different drummer. Let him step to the music which he hears, however measured or far away.

HENRY DAVID THOREAU

It was going to be a long day.

I knocked on the apartment door. It swung open. Roger was standing there, wearing a black shirt and an apron. He had a gold earring in his left ear.

"For crying out loud," my father said.

"Hi, Mom. Hey, Dad," Roger said. Then he rubbed my boys' heads and hugged my wife and hit me on the shoulder.

"Hey, brother."

Then he said, "I want you to meet Tiffany."

There she was. This woman who had led Roger astray, who had led him down the false path of vegetarianism. She was pale and thin. She had the sniffles. She trembled.

My mother took one look at Tiffany, and her mother gene kicked in. She said, "Oh, you poor thing, you're sick. Let's get you to bed."

She took Tiffany by the hand and led her through the front room, down the hallway and into the bedroom. We could hear my mother clucking. She came back into the front room.

"That poor child is anemic," she told us. "She's low on iron. This no-meat nonsense has got to stop. Roger, take me to the grocery. Now."

By that time my father was in the kitchen. He called out for me to come in. He was standing at the table.

"Can you believe this?" he said. "This is what they were gonna feed us. Will you look at this?"

There was macaroni without the cheese, and apples. Small, wormy apples. Pesticide-free apples. There was a plate of lettuce and a pitcher of herbal tea on the table, and a bowl of kiwi fruit.

"For crying out loud," my father said. "No wonder that girl's sick. She's starving to death."

My mother and Roger were back within the hour. They had a turkey breast, potatoes, cranberries, and a two-liter bottle of RC Cola. My mother put the turkey in the oven and began peeling the potatoes.

"This is more like it," my father said.

My mother arranged the food on the table. She went to get Tiffany. She took her by the arm and led her to the table.

Tiffany moaned, "I can't eat this. I'm a vegan."

My mother thumbed through her Bible to the book of Acts, chapter 10, and began to read, "And Peter became hungry and desired something to eat; but while they were preparing it, he fell into a trance and saw the heaven opened, and something descending, like a great sheet, let down by four corners upon the earth. In it were all kinds of animals. And there came a voice to him, 'Rise, Peter, kill and eat.'"

Then she closed her Bible and turned to Tiffany and said, "Well, Tiffany honey, there you have it. It doesn't get any clearer than that. Now eat up."

So Tiffany ate. Not much, but she did eat. And so did we, sitting around the table. Great slabs of turkey with mounds of mashed potatoes and cranberries. Heaven food. Manna. We washed it down with glasses of RC Cola.

The color began to rise in Tiffany's face. Her trembling stilled.

Roger needed no convincing. He had three helpings of turkey. He looked suspiciously robust for a vegetarian. His black shirt was stretched tight across his stomach. I began to suspect he'd been sneaking hamburgers.

Tiffany went to her room to do her yoga.

"She does her yoga after every meal," Roger told us. "Isn't she something!"

We all agreed that she was something.

I asked Roger how long he'd been a vegan.

He looked guilty. He lowered his voice. "Strictly speaking," he said, "I guess I'm not a total vegan."

He'd done it for Tiffany, he told us. She'd talked about it at the poetry reading, when they'd first met. She'd told him how she'd been meat-free for three weeks, and what a cleansing experience it was.

Roger had nodded and agreed, "Yes, it is cleansing, isn't it."

From that day forward, it had been macaroni without cheese, salads without dressing, and small, wormy apples. They'd eat at her apartment, then Roger would kiss her good-bye and drive past the Burger King for a Whopper. Then he'd go home and gargle Listerine to get the hamburger off his breath.

"Don't tell Tiffany," he said.

My father said, "Well, that's ridiculous. I'd never do that. I'd never put on airs just to get a woman to like me. That's for sure."

My mother snorted. "I don't even want to hear that. When we first met and you found out I was a Quaker, you claimed to be a Quaker too, just to get on my good side. So don't act so self-righteous."

She started laughing. "He even hid his car. He thought we were like the Amish, that we didn't drive cars."

Roger said, "For crying out loud."

Tiffany finished her yoga and came in and sat cross-legged next to Roger. She was feeling guilty for eating a piece of turkey. She felt defiled, like Peter. She ate some lettuce to cleanse her system.

My mother asked her what it meant to be a vegan. Tiffany said, "It like means you don't eat anything with a face. But it's like more than a diet. It's like being in harmony with like all of creation."

My mother smiled and nodded. She thought, Well, if they get married, I guess they won't be moving to Harmony and I guess Tiffany won't be helping with the Chicken Noodle Dinner.

She didn't say that, she just thought it.

*T*hen it was time to go. Roger and Tiffany walked us to the car. Roger rubbed my boys' heads and kissed my wife and punched me in the shoulder.

"Good-bye, brother."

He shook hands with my father and kissed my mother, who whispered in his ear, "I like your earring."

We got in the car and headed west, toward home. The sun was setting through the veiny trees. The boys fell asleep. It was quiet, except for the hum of the tires on the road.

My mother broke the silence. "I like Tiffany. She's a little different, but at least she's trying to do what she thinks is right. You got to give her credit for trying. What was that she said about being in harmony with all creation? That doesn't sound so wrong. Maybe we oughtta try that."

We drove on, pondering a no-meat future. A bleak prospect.

A few miles further, my father asked, "Why would a man wear an earring?"

"Probably for the same reason a man pretends to be a Quaker," I told him.

"For crying out loud," he said.

We don't think people will love us as we are, so we pretend to be someone we're not.

My father pretending to be a Quaker.

Roger making believe he's a vegan.

Wrinkled women lifting their faces, chasing their youth.

Fat men sucking in bellies.

Poor folks putting on airs.

Sinners acting like saints.

All of us keeping pace with our companions, stepping lively in this dance of deceit.

It is so hard, in this world, to be who we are.

My mother reached across and rubbed my father's shoulder. She said, "I'd have married you whether you were a Quaker or not."

"Really?" he asked.

"Really," she said.

"How come?" he asked.

"Because you're worth loving," she told him.

My father blushed.

"For crying out loud," he said. "For crying out loud."

Winter

Nineteen

Miriam and Ellis

When I was growing up at Harmony Friends Meeting, each family sat in the same pew every Sunday. My family sat on the right-hand side in the fifth row, in back of Ellis and Miriam Hodge and in front of Fern Hampton. We sat in that same place every Sunday morning, with never a deviation, on the off chance that if the Lord came during worship to take his children home, He would know right where to find us.

My wife and two sons sit there now, along with my mother and father, which makes for a snug fit. My wife and I considered having another child, then realized we'd need a bigger pew and didn't want to upset the fragile balance of the meeting. So our family is small, due to Quaker family planning—parents ought never bear more children than their pew can hold.

Some mornings, when the meetinghouse is empty, I'll sit in that fifth pew and say my prayers. When I was in seminary, the professors taught that God was omnipresent, that He was equally present in all places all the time. But they've never sat in that fifth row, so I consider theirs an uninformed opinion. That's where I've always found God, ever since I was a child.

Most children don't like church. Can't abide the silence, the sermon, the stillness. Their heads flop from side to side in rhythmic boredom. But I liked church. I liked sitting in the fifth row with my brother Roger and my parents and God, who sat right next to me. I liked watching Miriam Hodge. I liked her neck, how long it was, how wisps of hair fell against it. I liked watching Ellis Hodge plunge his index finger into a strand and curl it around his finger. How Miriam would turn and smile at him.

I was a morbid child, fascinated with stories of orphaned children having to stay with relatives. My Aunt Edna lived by herself in the next town over in a little house with window blinds which she kept closed. It was a dark, joyless place. She was my father's sister, a pinched-up woman. Once a summer, after church, we would drive the twelve miles to her house for dinner. It was pure obligation. We could barely endure it. Once my brother Roger stuck his finger down his throat and vomited on her shag carpet so we could leave early. When we got to the car, my father thanked him.

I tried to get along with Aunt Edna because I knew if something happened to my parents I'd have to live with her, even though I didn't want to. I wanted to live with Ellis and Miriam Hodge and asked my parents to write in their wills that I was to stay with them. They couldn't have children. Miriam Hodge talked about it once with my mother and began to weep.

They were sitting in our living room. I was hiding behind the couch, listening. I heard my mother say to her, "Believe me, Miriam, children are no picnic. They can drive you crazy."

It shocked me to hear that. I'd had no idea I was such a burden. I wondered if my father felt the same way. I worried about that. I worried about their taking me to Aunt Edna's house and leaving me there.

So Miriam and Ellis Hodge were a comfort to me. I could live with them. They loved me. Ellis Hodge carried jawbreakers in his pocket. If the sermon was especially tedious, he would reach back and tap my knee and drop a jawbreaker into my hand. I would suck all the color off and roll it in my mouth until it was gone. If it was silent, you could hear it clicking against my teeth.

*M*iriam and Ellis lived on a farm west of town. They were born two days apart and had grown up neighbors. When they were little, their families would joke about them growing up and marrying one another. They heard that joke so often that after a while Miriam and Ellis stopped laughing and thought Why not? and were married at the meetinghouse. Then, to their surprise, they found themselves very much in love. A few years later, Ellis's father died and Miriam and Ellis moved into the old Hodge house just west of town. They had a barn and a pond with ducks and a horse. I could be happy there.

But nothing happened to my parents, so I stayed with them until I graduated from high school and went to college. I came home during Christmas break and on Sunday morning sat on the fifth row, just behind the Hodges. Ellis slipped me a jawbreaker and Miriam asked about my studies and whether I had a girlfriend.

Ellis said, "Don't badger the boy. Let him play the field. I wish I would have. I married too soon. Yes sir, I did. I should have married Darlene Hughes. She inherited that big farm. Yes siree, I should have played the field."

Then he laughed. It was an old joke with them, Ellis marrying Darlene Hughes. Miriam would say, "Maybe you should have. But then when she found out what a terrible man you are, she'd have dumped you for good. That's for sure."

Only people who love each other can say these things. If these things are true, if they're actually felt, they can never be spoken. But if you've found your joy, if you've found your love, you can joke about what might have been, knowing life couldn't possibly be better. If you're Ellis Hodge, you joke about marrying Darlene Hughes, but at night you fall asleep thanking the good Lord for giving you Miriam instead.

I came home for spring break. Went to meeting. Miriam wasn't there. Ellis sat by himself in the fourth row. I asked after Miriam. He told me she wasn't feeling well. He was so consumed with her plight, he forgot to give me a jawbreaker.

*I*n May, my parents came to fetch me home for the summer. As we drove past Ellis and Miriam's farm, my mother turned from the front seat and said, "It's a terrible thing about Miriam Hodge. She has breast cancer. Ellis is just beside himself. They have to go up to the city for an operation and treatment. Pastor Taylor told about it last Sunday at church."

The next day was Sunday. Pastor Taylor asked if there were any prayer concerns. My father raised his hand and asked for prayers for Ellis and Miriam. Ellis reached over and pulled Miriam to him. I could see her shoulders shaking and could hear her soft weeping. Ellis swiped across his eyes with his arm. They were to go to the city that very week.

They didn't like the city. It scared them. They went only once a year, in December, to see the Christmas lights downtown. They drove their pickup truck and held fast in the right-hand lane. Doors locked. One year they ate lunch at a restaurant and it cost fifteen dollars, an outrageous sum. It ruined their day. After that, they packed their lunch and would eat it in the truck with the doors locked.

People would ask them why they went to see the Christmas lights in the daytime, that the lights showed up better at night.

Ellis would say, "You won't catch me in the city at night. No siree. Why, a fella could get killed up there. I watch TV. I read the newspaper. I know what happens. You won't get me up there at night."

So they'd go in the daytime and use their imaginations.

Then Miriam came down with cancer and Dr. Neely was sending her to a hospital in the city for an operation. They were terribly upset. Pastor Taylor prayed for them, then they sang "Abide with Me."

Miriam and Ellis left the next morning. They had to be there at noon. They left at eight o'clock, holding fast to the right-hand lane. They got turned around a few times and went the wrong way down a one-way street. Red-faced people honked their horns. Ellis didn't understand the principle behind a one-way street.

He said to Miriam, "What good is a street if you can't use it both ways? What are these people thinking of?"

They wanted to turn around, go home, and take their chances. But after a while they found the hospital and parked their truck and locked the doors. Ellis had read newspaper stories of cars being stolen in the city and didn't want their 1981 Ford pickup to be an easy target. They walked into the hospital and showed the lady behind the desk the piece of paper Dr. Neely had given them.

There was a man standing near the desk, looking at them. Ellis put his hand on his wallet. He'd read stories in the newspapers about people having their wallets stolen in the city. The lady called the man over and asked if he would be so kind to show Ellis and Miriam where they were to go.

The man asked them their names and told them his and asked what brought them to the hospital.

Ellis said, "It's my wife. She has the cancer. They'll be operating on her tomorrow." He could barely say it without crying.

The man asked, "Can I put you on the prayer list at our church so we can pray for you?"

Well, this shocked Ellis. He thought people in the city didn't pray, that they just took drugs and sat around in bars and fired guns at one another and unleashed pit bulls on small children. Then to meet this young man who wanted to pray for them—what a comfort that was.

They ran tests on Miriam all that day. That evening, they wheeled her into her room. She was tired and frightened. Ellis sat next to her, rubbing her hair, plunging in an index finger and twirling a lock of hair around it. He wanted to spend the night with her, in the chair next to her bed. But the nurse said he couldn't stay past visiting hours. This upset Ellis. They had been together every night for twenty years, and now this—absent the one night she needed him the most. He didn't know what to think.

The nurse told him of a place across the street where he could sleep for free. So that's where he went, and where he stayed for the next week while Miriam lay in the hospital.

He'd get up every morning and walk across the street, up the stairs to Miriam's room. He didn't trust elevators. He'd read stories in the newspaper of people being stuck on elevators for days at a time. Each day at noon, Ellis phoned Pastor Taylor with an update. Things were looking good, he reported. The doctors think they got it all. But she wasn't out of the woods yet. Keep praying.

Every evening, after visiting hours, he'd walk back across the street to his room. The first few nights he went straight to his room, then he took to lingering in the big room with all the other people. They'd talk about their loved ones being operated on across the way. They would cry, and sometimes they would laugh, and sometimes they would pray. They wrote their telephone numbers on slips of paper and promised to keep in touch. It was a great comfort to Ellis to visit with these people. It reminded him of church.

Some evenings a Catholic priest, Father Leopold, would visit. At first, Ellis was suspicious. He had never met a Catholic priest but had heard they drank wine, which was something good Christians did not do. But Father Leopold was a kind man, who always remembered Ellis's name and always asked about Miriam. After a while, Ellis thought maybe a little wine every now and then was no great sin.

The first night there, Ellis had gone to a grocery store and bought seven cans of ravioli. He loved ravioli in a can, but never got to eat it because Miriam didn't believe in eating food from cans. She worried that the metal fragments from opening the cans fell in the food and poisoned your body. Ellis missed his ravioli.

He ate ravioli every night for seven nights. On the last night, he invited Father Leopold to eat with him. Father Leopold brought a bottle of wine. They ate ravioli and drank red wine in Dixie cups from the bathroom.

The next morning it was time to go home. Ellis pulled the truck up to the hospital entrance. The nurse wheeled Miriam through the hospital and out the door and right up to the truck and hugged her and kissed her cheek and said, "You get better now. We'll be thinking of you."

Father Leopold was there. He prayed for Miriam and Ellis and rubbed a little holy water on their foreheads. Ellis worried all the way home that they'd been secretly baptized into the Catholic church. He'd read stories in the newspaper of that happening.

Once a month afterward, Miriam and Ellis drove up to the hospital for tests, then every six weeks, then every three months. Now, just once a year.

They've started breathing again. Relaxing. Sometimes whole days will pass with them forgetting.

One Sunday during prayer time, Ellis stood and talked about how God had always seemed especially near in the fourth row at Harmony Friends, but that now he knew better. Now he knew God was everywhere, even up in the city.

That night, he and Miriam were lying in bed like spoons, holding one another. Ellis was not a demonstrative man, was not a man given to flowery speech, but lying there next to his wife, he was overcome.

He said to her, "I love you more than anything. I'm glad you're better. I can't imagine life without you."

She said, "Oh, you'd have married Darlene Hughes and lived on that big farm. You'd have gotten over me pretty quick."

Then they laughed the gentle laugh of people in love.

Ellis said, "Say, this Christmas, why don't we drive up to the city and stay in one of those fancy hotels and see the Christmas lights at night? I bet they'd be pretty at night."

"Can we eat in a restaurant?" Miriam asked.

He said, "Why not? Let's live a little."

She said, "Yes, let's. Let's live a little."

Ellis and Miriam still live west of town on the old Hodge place, and every Sunday morning they sit in the fourth row at Harmony Friends Meeting. I'm their pastor now. If my sermon is a bit tedious, Ellis reaches back and taps my sons on their knees and slips them jawbreakers, which they suck down to nothing.

To look at Miriam and Ellis, you wouldn't think there was anything special about them. But love has a way of making ordinary people seem remarkable, and in that sense, Miriam and Ellis are the most fascinating people I know.

Twenty

Memory

"Walloped by Winter!" read the headline of *The Harmony Herald* the week of the December snowstorm. Underneath the headline was a picture of Pastor Taylor shoveling the steps of the Harmony Friends meetinghouse, where he had been the pastor. The picture was twenty-seven years old, taken during the last big snowstorm to hit Harmony. Pastor Taylor was now dead, but Bob Miles Jr. was loath to spend money on new pictures if a suitable photograph could be found in the files. So there was Pastor Taylor, resurrected and noticeably slimmer, shoveling snow.

In the foreground was a 1972 Plymouth Valiant. Pastor Taylor had loved that car. He was two years out of seminary when he came to Harmony, his wife was pregnant, and he drove a Volkswagen Beetle—a foreign car, which had not endeared him to his congregation. So in March of 1973, when he drove by Harvey Muldock's car dealership and saw the '72 Valiant sitting there, Pastor Taylor turned into Harvey's lot on impulse.

Harvey had written *DEEP DISCOUNT!!!* with white shoe polish on the front windshield and taped a small American flag to the antenna, which had caught Pastor Taylor's eye. He pulled alongside the Valiant, climbed from his Volkswagen, and there was Harvey, his hand extended, his smile a bit too big. It had been a slow month for Harvey and taxes were coming due.

Harvey walked around the front of the Valiant, raised the hood and proclaimed, "She has a slant-six engine with two hundred and twenty-five horse. Best engine ever made. It's the last one on the lot. I'll let you have it for three thousand dollars."

Pastor Taylor gazed at the motor, trying to think of something knowledgeable to say. He opened the car door and the smell of new car rose to greet him. Gray vinyl seats, with ridges. AM radio. Seat belts snug on clips above the windows. What a beauty. But three thousand dollars…

He eased himself behind the steering wheel. Closed his eyes and inhaled the smell. Oh, such a car. His wife was pregnant. He thought of his baby riding in a nice car like this, instead of in the old Volkswagen.

Pastor Taylor had seventy-eight dollars in his savings account.

"Too rich for my blood," he said, then stepped out and shook Harvey's hand good-bye. He climbed in his Volkswagen, now shabby in comparison, and drove home to the parsonage.

*T*he next week it snowed twelve inches, and when Pastor Taylor was shoveling the steps of the meetinghouse, Bob Miles Jr. of the *Herald* pulled up in his new car, a 1972 Plymouth Valiant, parked in front of the meetinghouse, stood on the opposite sidewalk, and snapped a picture of Pastor Taylor shoveling snow with the Valiant in the foreground.

Then he crossed the street and Pastor Taylor said, "That's quite a car you have there, Bob Jr."

Bob Jr. said, "Harvey made me a real deal on it. It was the last '72 on the lot. Three thousand, three hundred dollars."

"Well, you certainly know how to bargain," Pastor Taylor told him. "I ought to take you with me the next time I buy a car. That's some deal. I don't see how Harvey can stay in business making those kinds of deals."

Most men would have laughed at Bob Jr. Most men would have said, "I had Harvey down to three thousand," but not Pastor Taylor. He could not preach very well. He was not very creative but he was exceedingly kind, which explained his survival. He served twenty-seven years as the pastor of Harmony Friends Meeting. A church record. Fourteen hundred sermons, not one of them memorable. But he was loved and that was his legacy.

His first child, a daughter, was born three weeks after the 1973 snowstorm. The doctor's bill came to seventy-five dollars, which left three dollars in Pastor Taylor's savings account, which he spent on spark plugs for the Volkswagen and a roll of duct tape to patch the seats.

He never owned a new car. Once a year he would drive to Harvey's dealership and smell the new cars, but he could never afford one. We never paid him enough. All those years of sacrifice, then struck down while jogging on the eve of retirement. We were going to buy him a new car for his retirement, then to be struck by a car and killed. What irony. Life is so unfair. Why couldn't Dale Hinshaw have been hit by the car?

When I became pastor, it was Dale Hinshaw who called to say it would be my job to shovel the walk and spread the salt. I told him I hadn't gone to seminary so I could shovel snow. That was when he quoted from the book of James that faith without works is dead. Dale Hinshaw knew just enough Scripture to be annoying but not enough to be transformed.

He was all the time talking about how Pastor Taylor did things: "Pastor Taylor cooked for the men's breakfasts" or "Pastor Taylor came to see us once a month" or "Pastor Taylor never complained about shoveling the walk."

After our big December snowstorm it was Dale Hinshaw who cut out the old picture of Pastor Taylor shoveling snow and thumbtacked it to the meetinghouse bulletin board, a serious breach of protocol. The bulletin board was administered by the Friendly Women's Circle. Before my grandmother died, the church bulletin board had been her responsibility as president of the circle. Once a month they met to change it. People in the meeting were free to offer bulletin board suggestions, which the Friendly Women's Circle would vote on and then make using construction paper and pictures from magazines. There were Christmas themes and Easter bulletin boards. Their summer vacation bulletin board had proclaimed, *"That my joy may be in you, and your joy might be full."* It showed a family playing volleyball and waterskiing. Everyone was smiling. It didn't look like any vacation I'd ever taken.

Then there was the bulletin board Dale Hinshaw had suggested, which his wife rammed through the Friendly Women's Circle. It read, *Don't Retire in the Lake of Fire.* It had a picture of tormented souls screaming amidst a ball of flame. One of the tormented souls looked suspiciously like my grandmother, whom Mrs. Dale Hinshaw had not particularly cared for ever since the women of the Friendly Circle voted her out as president and my grandmother in.

I loved my grandmother, and when she died from a stroke I was beyond consoling. I had gone to visit her one morning and had let myself in. She never locked her doors. I once asked her why and she told me someone might need to get in, which they wouldn't be able to do if the door was locked. Because she felt no malice toward anyone, she never suspected it from others. It's the suspicious people who get preyed upon the most.

I remember one morning pushing open her door and calling her name. There was no reply, no slight laugh, no "Come in, Sam." Just

silence. I found her in bed, cold to the touch. I called my p
Mackey's Funeral Home, then sat beside her and smoothed
wanted her to look her best. Pretty soon my mother and fat
then Johnny Mackey with his hearse.

That was eight years ago, but when anything happens to n
I ought to call Grandma and tell her. Then I remember and
over again.

Pastor Taylor presided at her funeral. I can't recall a thin
What I do recollect is my brother Roger and me walkin
Grandma's house, room by room, dividing her earthly goods.
my grandfather made so Grandma could reach the punchbo
top cabinet. The cast-iron doorstop that propped open the f
The cookie jar with the rooster on it that I remember reachi
a child. It was high up on the counter; I had to stand on th
grandfather made.

I wanted it all, as if by surrounding myself with her thin
keep her alive. I wanted to touch the things she had touched.
turn off the kitchen light and stood there wondering how n
Grandma had touched that very switch. My finger lingered th
ering connection to that saintly woman.

I thought of this as I shoveled the church walk, thoug
uncertain life was and how having Grandma around h
to calm the whirlwind. Grandma sitting in that same d
the same old meetinghouse in the same old town. Then wall
down the same old sidewalk, careful not to stumble where
tree had heaved up the concrete. Cooked Sunday dinner at th
stove and fed us on the same old Sunday china.

Then I thought of Dale Hinshaw and my anger fell a
more alike than we are different. We're both holding on to th

more, both wanting what used to be. So when he opened the *Herald*
 there was Pastor Taylor from 1973, it took him back and brought
 n peace. And he thought if it brought him peace, it would do the same
 others. So he clipped it out and thumbtacked it to the church bul-
 n board.

It's still there. The Friendly Women's Circle wanted to take it down
 put up a Christmas bulletin board, but I asked them to leave it up a
 ile longer. I told them that sometimes all we have is memory, that
 netimes it's all that gets us through, and we ought be really careful
 ore letting it go.

Twenty-one
The Spelling Bee

For the past thirty years, *The Harmony Herald* has sponsored the local spelling bee for the kids in the sixth grade. I was in Miss Fishbeck's class in the sixth grade. She would divide the class in half, the boys against the girls. The girls would line up in front of the chalkboard, underneath the picture of George Washington. The boys would stand against the back wall between the globe and the fish tank. There was a sea of shiny, wood floor between us, which Mr. Griswold, the janitor, polished the week before school and the week after Christmas.

Miss Fishbeck would stand in the center of the room calling out words like *epistle* and *cameo* and *demeanor*. Words we boys never used. The words we did use, being sixth-grade boys, were never called in a spelling bee, so we were always at a disadvantage and the girls would invariably win. If Miss Fishbeck had called out words like *booger* and *poop* the boys could have won; but she never did, so we were doomed from the start.

The winner of our class would then take on the winners from the other sixth-grade classes. The school champion would proceed to the County Spelling Bee, then that winner would go to the state championship, whose winner would move on to the national competition in

Washington, D.C. If you won the National Spelling Bee, you got to visit the White House and have your picture taken with the president of the United States of America.

I dreamed about that. I dreamed of outspelling Muriel Burgdorf and getting my picture in the *Herald*. Then winning the County Spelling Bee. Then going to the state capital and staying the night in a hotel and spelling the word *lipopolysaccharide* and traveling to Washington, D.C., and winning the National Spelling Bee and shaking hands with Richard Nixon, who would spend an entire day with me, showing me the secret tunnels under the White House and shooting baskets with me in the White House gym.

But it was not to be. Miss Fishbeck called out the word *receive* and I forgot the cardinal rule of spelling bees: *i* before *e* except after *c,* or when sounded as a long *a* as in *neighbor* or *weigh*. But Muriel Burgdorf didn't forget, so she won and had her picture put in the *Herald*. She went on to the county fair, where she blew it. She spelled the word *miscellaneous,* a hard word, then stumbled on the word *Mississippi,* which, despite its length, was an easy word to spell. It was the word you prayed would be called when it was your turn to spell.

I remembered how to spell *Mississippi* by imagining Miss Fishbeck sipping a drink. Miss is sipping. You just had to remember to stop at the *n,* which Muriel forgot to do. She burst into tears. We looked away, embarrassed, as Miss Fishbeck led her from the stage, both of them weeping.

That was the best our school had ever done until Amanda Hodge moved here this last summer.

Amanda is the niece of Miriam and Ellis Hodge. She is the daughter of Ellis's youngest brother, Ralph, who is a waste of flesh according to Ellis, who seldom has a bad word to say about anyone. So when Ellis does get around to saying something bad about someone, you are inclined to believe him.

*I*t was a cruel joke—how Ralph and his wife, drunkards both, could conceive and bear such a beautiful child, while Ellis and Miriam Hodge, who worked hard and went to church every Sunday, remained barren. Ellis had brought up the matter several times with God, but had not yet received a satisfactory explanation.

Ralph and his wife had lived away from Harmony most of their married life. Then Ralph was fired from his job, and he and his wife came back to Harmony to work on the family farm. The only reason Ellis let him was because of Amanda. They showed up one night, reeking of whiskey. Ellis wanted to turn them away, and would have except for the little girl standing between them. Instead, he bought a doublewide trailer, set it in the field, furnished it, then told his brother, "This is it, Ralph. This is your last chance. If you don't knock off the booze, you'll have to leave."

But it was an empty threat and Ralph knew it. He knew Ellis and Miriam couldn't bear the thought of him and his wife moving away and taking Amanda with them. So Ellis fumed and threatened, but in the end, did nothing. Except every Saturday morning, Ellis and Miriam would bring Amanda to their house for the weekend. They would take her fishing at the pond, or to the Dog 'n' Suds in the next town over for a root beer, then would have her spend the night. They ordered pink sheets from the Sears catalog. Amanda picked them out herself. They bought her a white bed with a canopy and set it up in their guest room and told her it would be her room as long as she wanted it.

On Sunday mornings, Miriam would make Amanda's favorite breakfast, blueberry pancakes, and they would go to meeting. They would sit on the fourth row. Ellis and Amanda sitting like bookends around Miriam, leaning into her.

After church, they would go home and eat Sunday dinner and then snap beans on the porch or play pitch and catch. They'd play word games. Miriam would thumb through the dictionary, calling out words for Amanda to spell. Then Miriam would braid Amanda's hair. They'd sit on the porch steps—Amanda on the bottom step with Miriam on the step above her, dividing her hair into two strands of threes and braiding them. They'd put off taking Amanda home as long as they could. Then, after dinner, Ellis and Miriam would walk her home. They'd walk slowly, prolonging their bliss.

They lived for Saturday mornings, when Ellis would hike across the field to the trailer and tap on the door and ask, "Can we borrow your little sweetie for the weekend?" Twice, Ralph and his wife said no because they liked watching Ellis sag when he heard that word. They liked the power of it. They were that kind of people.

Then Ellis got Ralph alone in the barn and told him, "If you ever keep us from Amanda again, we'll call the police and report you for neglect and you'll go to jail." He felt terrible saying that. He felt like a bully. But he and Miriam loved that girl so much. They even talked with Ralph and his wife about adopting her.

Ralph said, "It'll cost you fifty thousand dollars. Not a dime less." They were that kind of people.

When fall came, Amanda entered the sixth grade and was assigned to Miss Fishbeck's class. It was Miss Fishbeck's last year to teach. She was retiring. Her only regret was that in all her years of teaching, she'd never had a County Spelling Bee champion. It nagged at her. Every year she divided the classroom in half—girls up front underneath George Washington, boys in back by the fish tank—and would drill them. It was a discouragement. The boys would put the *e* before the *i*. The girls would collapse under the least pressure.

After all these years, Miss Fishbeck had learned not to expect much.

She had gotten her hopes up with Muriel Burgdorf, only to be crushed. She'd learned her lesson: Expect nothing. Then here came Amanda Hodge, standing at the chalkboard, spelling every word Miss Fishbeck threw her way. She started out easy—*ankle* and *adverb* and *confuse.* Amanda spelled them without blinking, clearly and with confidence.

Miss Fishbeck grew mildly excited. She called out *iniquity.* Amanda spelled it.

Miss Fishbeck began breathing faster. *"Lacerate,"* she said. "Can you spell *lacerate?"*

"Lacerate," repeated Amanda. *"L-a-c-e-r-a-t-e. Lacerate."*

Miss Fishbeck trembled. Who was this child? Where had she come from? She went for broke. *"Labyrinthian,"* she said.

Amanda smiled and said, "I know that one. *Labyrinthian. L-a-b-y-r-i-n-t-h-i-a-n. Labyrinthian.* That's easy."

Miss Fishbeck began to weep.

They had spelling bees every day for a week. Amanda never missed a word—*lactiferous, conductance,* and *polyribonucleotide.*

A month later it was time for the sixth-grade spell-off, which Amanda won. Bob Miles Jr. took her picture for the *Herald.* Ellis and Miriam took her to the Dog 'n' Suds for a root beer. The next month was the County Spelling Bee. Miss Fishbeck sat on the front row, her Bible clutched in her hands, praying the Lord's Prayer, lingering on "Thy will be done."

It came down to Amanda and a boy from Cartersburg.

The caller looked at the boy and said, *"Colloquialism."* The boy hesitated at the second *l,* screwed his eyes in thought, and left it out.

The caller turned to Amanda. *"Colloquialism,"* she said.

"Colloquialism," Amanda repeated. *C-o-l-l-o-q-u-i-a-l-i-s-m. Colloquialism."* Miss Fishbeck let out a gasp and clutched her Bible to her chest.

Then Amanda spelled the word *lackadaisical* and it was over.

Pandemonium. Miss Fishbeck ran up the steps, no small feat, and hugged Amanda to her and that was the picture Bob Miles snapped for the *Herald*. Ellis and Miriam stood beaming on the first row. Ralph and his wife weren't there.

*A*manda went on to the State Spelling Bee. Miss Fishbeck took the entire sixth grade on a school bus all the way to the state capitol building. Ellis and Miriam followed in their truck, with Bob Miles Jr. sandwiched between them. They parked in front of a fire hydrant and Bob put a big card on the windshield that read *PRESS*. Bob had always wanted to do that.

The governor himself called out the words for the spelling bee. It went on for three hours, kids dropping like flies, all the way down to Amanda and two other girls. It was painful to watch—a spelling-bee holocaust. The two girls were trembling with fear. Too much pressure. They went down.

The governor turned to Amanda.

"Quintuplicate," he declared.

"Quintuplicate," repeated Amanda. *"Q-u-i-n-t-u-p-l-i-c-a-t-e. Quintuplicate."*

And that was it.

This was in October. The National Spelling Bee wasn't until January. Every Saturday, Amanda came to Ellis and Miriam's house. Miriam would read words from the dictionary and Amanda would spell them. They'd go for drives through the country. Ellis would point out trees, then pull the truck over and look them up in the tree book he carried in his glovebox.

"There's an oak tree," he'd say. "Its scientific name is *Lithocarpus*."

"Lithocarpus," Amanda would repeat. *"L-i-t-h-o-c-a-r-p-u-s. Lithocarpus."*

"Atta girl," he'd say.

On the Friday after Christmas, they drove up to the city to see the Christmas lights, and spent the night in a hotel. That Sunday they returned to Harmony and went to meeting. I was on vacation and had invited a professor from my old seminary to bring a message. It was entitled "The Hermeneutics of Suspicion." He talked about how it is we know what we know and whether we can be sure we really know it. People smiled as he spoke, not understanding a word he was saying. Not even Amanda understood, though she was enthralled with the word *hermeneutics*. What a fascinating word! She wondered what it meant and how to spell it.

Dale Hinshaw thought it was a man's name. "Herman Uticks. He must be one of them German fellas," he speculated the next day at the Coffee Cup.

After Sunday dinner, Amanda looked it up in Miriam's dictionary. *Hermeneutics: the study of the methodological principles of interpretation.* She still wasn't sure what it meant. She'd have to ask Miss Fishbeck. Miss Fishbeck would know. Miss Fishbeck knew everything.

*T*he National Spelling Bee was held in the middle of January in Washington, D.C. Harvey Muldock loaned Miriam and Ellis a brand-new car for the trip. Bob Miles Jr. from the *Herald* was Amanda's press entourage, plus when Ellis got tired, he drove. Miss Fishbeck and Miriam and Amanda sat in the backseat, spelling words. It was the farthest any of them had ever traveled. They left on a Sunday, early. By ten that morning they'd crossed the Ohio River, then drove over the Appalachians and into the Shenandoah Valley. They drove twelve hours, then pulled into the parking lot of the Grand Hyatt on H Street, where the spelling bee contestants were staying.

They all shared a room. Ellis and Bob Jr. in one bed, Miss Fishbeck and Miriam in the other, and Amanda on a roll-out cot by the window. When they first arrived, Ellis had stood at the door memorizing the fire escape instructions and reading the sign on the door that told how much the room cost. They hadn't told him at the front desk and he hadn't asked for fear of appearing cheap.

Two hundred and twelve dollars! He was about to complain, about ready to check out and go somewhere else, but he didn't want to make Amanda feel bad so he kept quiet. This was her day. To heck with the money.

When they had checked in downstairs, a man had offered to carry their suitcases upstairs, but Ellis didn't want to pay the man fifty cents, so he carried them himself. Miriam had brought along bread and bologna. They ate in the room, sitting on the beds, watching television. Sixty-seven channels. They watched Lawrence Welk.

The next morning they woke up, ate breakfast, climbed in the car and drove down H Street to Ninth Street, turned left, and pulled up to the Washington Convention Center. They made their way inside. Miss Fishbeck held her Bible to her chest, repeating the Lord's Prayer. Bob Miles carried his camera. Ellis and Miriam were sick with worry. They tried not to show it, but it couldn't be helped. The National Spelling Bee!

Amanda was the picture of calm.

It lasted five hours. By then, Ellis had sweated through his shirt onto his suit jacket. Miss Fishbeck had moved on to the Twenty-third Psalm: "Even though I walk through the valley of the shadow of death, I fear no evil, for thou art with me…" Each time Amanda spelled a word, Bob Jr. snapped her picture.

It came down to Amanda and a boy from Hawaii.

It was the boy's turn.

"Hendecasyllabic," the caller called. The boy studied the ceiling, then the floor, then began to spell. He forgot the second *l*.

But Amanda didn't. She was one word from victory.

Ellis and Miriam didn't breathe. This was it. By now, Miss Fishbeck was praying aloud.

"Hermeneutics," the caller declared.

Miss Fishbeck groaned. Miriam brightened. Bob Jr. whispered to Ellis, "Who's that?"

"Hermeneutics," Amanda said. *"H-e-r-m-e-n-e-u-t-i-c-s. Hermeneutics."*

Then the caller smiled and Ellis and Miriam breathed and Miss Fishbeck began to weep and Bob Jr. snapped a picture of Amanda receiving her trophy. Then everyone stood and clapped, even the boy from Hawaii.

*T*he next day they went to the White House, to the Oval Office, to shake hands with the president of the United States of America.

They were all there—Amanda and Miriam and Ellis, plus Miss Fishbeck and Bob Jr. The president stood with his arm around Amanda while Bob took their picture for the *Herald*.

Then the president turned to Miriam and Ellis and said, "These must be your parents. I bet you're proud of your daughter."

Ellis has never told a lie. But in that split second, it occurred to him that biology didn't make you a parent, love did. So Ellis stepped forward and shook the president's hand and said, "We couldn't be more proud."

"What was the winning word?" the President asked.

"Hermeneutics," said Amanda.

"Ah, yes, the study of the methodological principles of interpretation," he said.

"That's right," Amanda said. "I learned about it at church."

"That must be some church," the president said.

*T*hey drove back to Harmony the next day. Bob Miles Jr. dropped Miriam and Ellis and Amanda off at the farmhouse, where Amanda spent the night. They had blueberry pancakes for breakfast, then Ellis walked her home across the field.

Ralph and his wife were sitting at the kitchen table, bleary-eyed.

"I did it," Amanda told them. "I won. I won the National Spelling Bee."

She showed them her trophy.

Ralph turned, scratching his gut, and said, "Did you get any money?"

Amanda said, "No, but I got to meet the president."

Ralph snorted. "Don't let it go to your head." Then he said, "The dishes need doin'. Get on 'em."

*T*hat's when Ellis snapped. He took Amanda by the hand and walked her back across the field, back to the farmhouse to Miriam. He climbed in the truck and drove into town to the bank and cashed in their CDs, all the money they had in the world—thirty thousand dollars.

The manager was nervous. "Are you sure about this, Ellis?" he asked.

Ellis looked him in the eye and said, "I want it in fifties."

Then he drove back to the trailer. He didn't knock. He laid the money on the table in front of Ralph. He said, "There's thirty thousand dollars here. It's yours. But if you take this money, I never want to see you again. Amanda stays with us. When you're settled, mail me your address and I'll have the lawyer, Owen Stout, send you the papers. I'll send you five thousand dollars a year until Amanda turns eighteen. If you ever come back here, if you so much as step one foot in this town, the money stops. I want you out of here by tomorrow noon."

Ralph stared at the cash, then reached out and dragged the money across the table toward him. He looked at his wife and said, "Let's go see your sister in California."

Ellis didn't tell Miriam until that night. How do you tell your wife that you're now parents, without a dime to your name? He waited until the lights were out before telling her what he had done.

"I had to do it," Ellis said. "I couldn't bear the thought of that sweet child staying with them even one more night."

Miriam reached across and held him. "You did the right thing," she told him. "I love that girl. And there's things more important than money. We'll be fine."

Ralph and his wife left the next morning. Ellis and Miriam and Amanda watched from the kitchen window. Watched Ralph and his wife carry the last box to their car and close the trunk, watched them climb in their car and drive down the lane.

Ellis said to Amanda, "You'll be staying with us from now on. Your mother and father are going away. Is that all right?"

Amanda wasn't sure how to feel. She thought she should be sad, but she wasn't. She didn't even cry. That worried Miriam and Ellis.

They held her and said, "It's okay to cry, you know."

She said, "I know." But she didn't.

"If you ever want to talk about it, you can," Ellis told her.

Amanda said, "Okay."

Then Ellis said, "Hey, let's go play pitch and catch."

Miriam watched them from the kitchen window over the sink. She was a mother now. She'd always wanted to be a mom. Now that she was, she was scared. She wasn't sure how to be a parent. On top of that, they were broke. Ralph had all their money. Plus five thousand dollars a year. Where would they ever find that much money? But looking out the window at Ellis and Amanda playing pitch and catch, seeing Amanda catch a pop fly and hearing Ellis say "Atta girl," Miriam didn't feel broke. She felt blessed.

Blessed. B-l-e-s-s-e-d. Blessed.

Twenty-two

The Testimony

I t was late winter when Bob Miles Jr. first noticed the workers going in and out of the Harold Morrison building. He speculated about it in "The Bobservation Post" column for the *Herald:* "Lots of activity at the Harold Morrison building. Wonder what's going on?"

People all over town read that, then laid down their *Heralds* and remembered back to when Harold Morrison owned and operated the Morrison's Menswear shop on the town square. Harold Morrison died when I was twelve years old; the building has sat unused ever since. His widow never cleaned it out. You can still walk past and see the circular racks of work shirts and the suits and plaid sport jackets hanging against the west wall, now covered with a fine dust.

Across the back of the store was the shoe department. Harold sold Red Wing boots for the men and Red Goose shoes for the boys, made by the International Shoe Company of St. Louis, Missouri. He had a big red goose perched on the counter which laid a golden egg whenever a pair of Red Goose shoes were sold. I remember my mother taking my brother Roger and me to his store the first week of September for Harold's annual back-to-school sale. If you bought two pairs of pants, three shirts, three pairs of socks, and one pair of Red Goose shoes, Harold would throw in a package of Fruit of the Loom underwear for free.

We would always go in the afternoon because Harold would only sell shoes in the afternoon, when your feet were biggest. People had bought shoes in the morning, when their feet were small, and two weeks later returned them for a refund. So Harold posted a sign on the wall:

No shoes will be sold before 2:00 P.M.

At two o'clock, he would take the Brannock device down from the nail on the wall and start measuring feet. You'd stand straight up while Harold wrestled your foot into the Brannock device and measured its length and width. Then you would pick the shoe you wanted, which was not a complicated procedure. You had two decisions—brown or black, and low-cut or high-cut.

The best part came after your mother paid for the shoes. That's when Harold let you reach up and grab hold of the goose's head and pull it downward. You'd hear the golden egg rumble through the goose, a goose with indigestion, then the goose would lift her head and lay the golden egg.

Since we got only one egg a year, it was easy to forget what was in there. The real joy was holding the golden egg in your hand and imagining its contents. The opening was anticlimactic. A couple pieces of hard candy, a stick of bubble gum, a plastic cowboy, and a fake one-dollar bill.

Roger would open his egg while we were still in the store. But I would keep mine next to my bed, sometimes for weeks at a time, before twisting it open. It drove Roger mad. He would offer to trade for it, but I never would. When I'd open it, it was such a letdown. All that waiting, all that savoring, for some hard candy and a plastic toy.

According to Harold, the International Shoe Company of St. Louis, Missouri, had filled one golden egg with genuine gold coins, which had never been found. Whenever you'd pull down the goose head, Harold would say, "This might be the one." But it never happened in our town, or I'd have read about it in the *Herald*: "Local Boy Hits Jackpot."

That's why I would wait before opening the egg. I'd shake it once a day to see if it sounded like gold coins. I'd shake it just before bedtime, then go to sleep dreaming of the things I would buy if I ever hit the jackpot.

I had it all figured out.

I'd buy my mother a dishwasher. I'd buy my father a drill press. I'd give 10 percent to the church. Not because I was religious, but because my parents would make me. I was not devout as a child, knowing I had a lifetime to get back on God's good side. Now that I'm older, my walk of faith is more cautious. It doesn't pay to make God mad when you could check out any day. Now I would give 10 percent to the church without being told.

I would spend the rest of my money on a bicycle. A Schwinn Sting-Ray with a banana seat and a car steering wheel for handlebars. Then Harold Morrison died and there went the dishwasher, drill press, and banana seat bicycle.

Bob Miles Jr. first noticed the workers cleaning out the building when he walked past the Morrison building and saw them carrying out the red goose and lay it in Mabel Morrison's car trunk. He wondered if there were any golden eggs still in the goose. Maybe that egg with the gold coins was in there. Maybe someone else wondered the very same thing and would follow the widow Morrison home and steal the red goose and she would recognize them and they would have to kill her. Maybe hit her on the head with the red goose and knock her dead.

The thought of that brought a smile to Bob Jr.'s face. It would make a fascinating headline: "Local Woman Killed by Goose." Bob grew mildly excited at the prospect of writing about a murder. We'd never had a murder for him to write about. He thought it would be a test of his journalistic skills. But Mabel Morrison made it home and had some neighbor boys carry the red goose up to the attic and store it next to the box of Christmas decorations.

So Bob Miles is having to write about something else, which these days has not been hard. Someone from Harmony won the big lottery—five million dollars. We weren't sure who for nearly eight months, because the winner waited to turn in the winning ticket. The only thing we knew was that it was someone from the Harmony Friends Meeting. We did know that. Back in the summer Harvey Muldock got the idea to put a lottery ticket in each church bulletin to increase attendance. He went to the gas station out near the interstate and bought forty tickets, and one of them was the winner.

When one among you is a millionaire, but you're not sure who, you treat everyone with kindness on the off chance he or she is the winner and will think of you with fondness and, in a fit of gratitude, share the wealth. I personally know that on three occasions Fern Hampton wanted to tell off certain people, but held her tongue.

The lottery has done for our church what one hundred and seventy-five years of preaching could not—that is, cause us to treat one another with Christian charity. So I wasn't at all anxious for the winner to come forward. I wanted the winner to wait until the very last day to cash in the winning ticket.

For a while we thought Dale Hinshaw had won it. He'd sit on his porch looking at catalogs and when people wandered by and asked him what he was reading, he'd become guarded and secretive. He'd say, "Oh nothing, nothing at all," as he hid the catalog behind his back.

Dale subscribed to the *Wall Street Journal* and would read it at the

Coffee Cup, in plain view. Every now and again, lowering the paper and grinning a pleased grin.

Then he started talking about selling his old car and buying a new one. He went over to Harvey Muldock's car dealership and asked Harvey if there was a discount for paying cash. Then he said he wanted to think it over a little while, that he wanted to look at some other cars, maybe even go to the city to test drive a Mercedes.

But what really got people talking about Dale winning was when the Dale Hinshaws invited Ellis and Miriam Hodge over for Sunday dinner and he had travel brochures spread out on the dining room table.

Ellis said, "You and the missus thinking of taking a trip, Dale?"

Dale scooped up the brochures and said, "Oh, you never know. We just might."

Harvey Muldock and I talked about it. He didn't think Dale was the winner. He pointed out how Dale had gone out of his way to be nice to everyone. If Dale had been the winner, he'd have been his usual annoying self, plus a little worse, Harvey said. He thought Dale was faking it so people would be nice to him.

Then in early fall, Jessie Peacock came to my office. She was anxious. She sat across from me, her purse in her lap.

"Pastor, I have a matter of a confidential nature to discuss," she said.

This intrigued me. One benefit of being a pastor was discussing matters of a confidential nature. I leaned forward in my chair.

"How can I help you, Jessie?" I inquired.

She reached into her purse, pulled out a small slip of paper, and handed it to me across the desk. It was a lottery ticket.

Jessie said, "It's the winning ticket. It was in my bulletin. No one knows but me and Asa. I'll trust you not to tell anyone."

I was stunned. Five million dollars!

he only problem was that Jessie Peacock hated the lottery. The very Sunday the tickets were in the bulletins, she had stood during the silence to speak against the lottery. She thought the lottery was immoral. She thought the government should be ashamed of itself for encouraging its citizens to gamble. She'd gone to the library to research the lottery on the Internet.

"Did you know that 95 percent of the people who win the lottery end up wishing they'd never won it?" she told me.

"Did you know that 83 percent of the couples who win the lottery divorce?" she went on.

"Did you know that 68 percent of the people who win the lottery declare bankruptcy?" she asked.

I told her I wasn't aware of that.

"I despise the lottery," she said. "But Asa and I sure could use a nest egg. It's been hard times, and we're not getting any younger. We have ten thousand dollars set aside for our retirement. That's it. That's all we've been able to save in thirty years. And we didn't even save it. We got it when my daddy died."

She clutched her purse in her lap and worried at the strap.

I said, "Jessie, I can't tell you what to do. You'll have to figure that out yourself. You need to pray about it. I can't even imagine winning the lottery. I don't know what I'd do myself."

That wasn't true. I did know. I had it all figured out. I had gotten my lottery ticket from the bulletin the same Sunday and they didn't announce the numbers until the next Friday. That week I'd fallen asleep each night dreaming what I'd do if I won five million dollars. It was the golden egg all over again.

I had talked with my wife about it, lying in bed. She asked me what I'd buy if I won five million dollars.

"I've always wanted to buy my mother a dishwasher. I'd probably do that."

"That's it?" she asked. "That's all you'd buy?"

"Of course not," I told her. "I'd buy my father a drill press."

I had it all figured out.

Now here sat Jessie Peacock in my office with the winning ticket. She said, "I've half a mind to throw it away."

Instead, Jessie and Asa kept that ticket through fall and most of winter. They still hadn't made up their minds. They despised the lottery. They thought what it did to people was evil. But was it bad stewardship to turn down five million dollars? Was it even legal? Would they have to accept the money? They weren't sure.

Jessie broke in late winter. She stood at worship, during the silence, and asked for prayer for a personal problem. This perked people up considerably. They were hoping she'd elaborate, but she didn't. She just sat down, her face in her hands.

People sat in their pews, speculating.

Dale Hinshaw was thinking, Jessie and Asa are having marriage problems.

Fern Hampton was thinking, Jessie's dying. I just know it. She's got the cancer.

I was thinking what our meeting could do with the tithe on five million dollars.

*T*hat Tuesday morning, Jessie and Asa drove into town to talk with the lawyer, Owen Stout. Maybe Owen could help.

Bob Miles Jr. spied them from the front window of the *Herald* as he was writing "The Bobservation Post." He wrote, "Jessie and Asa Peacock are up and about early, visiting with the lawyer Stout."

Three days later, Dale Hinshaw was reading the paper. He said to his wife, "Yep, I was right. Looks like Jessie and Asa are getting a divorce."

Owen Stout wasn't much help. Assuming they were there to write their wills, he had already begun to fill out the forms when Jessie pulled the ticket from her purse and laid it on Owen's desk. His eyes bugged out and he offered to drive them to the city to the state lottery commission office.

He said, "You'll need a good lawyer. I can help you. You can pay me by the hour or just pay me a flat-out fee, say 10 percent. I think that's fair, don't you?"

Owen Stout was figuring the numbers in his head. Ten percent of five million dollars was half a million dollars. Yes, that sounded fair.

Jessie was talking, asking whether they had to accept the money. Owen wasn't listening. He was trying to figure out the taxes on half a million dollars. Probably about 40 percent. That would leave three hundred thousand dollars. He began to quiver.

He asked them, "Did you know that 92 percent of the people who win the lottery never hire a lawyer, and later wish they had?"

Asa and Jessie weren't aware of that.

The next week, Jessie came to my office. I asked her if she'd made up her mind.

She smiled and said, "I've decided to make a testimony." She told me what she had planned. I asked if Asa was in agreement. He was.

She called the state lottery commission from my office phone. Gave them her name. Read off the numbers. Told them she'd be in the next day to collect her money.

She and Asa left early the next morning and drove to the statehouse in the city. They walked into the rotunda. Television crews were setting up their lights. A man stood in the center dispensing orders.

Jessie approached him and stuck out her hand. "I'm Jessie Peacock. Are you in charge here?" she asked.

He brightened. "Oh yes, Mrs. Peacock. Congratulations! What a wonderful day this is for you. I bet you've been looking forward to this." Jessie smiled sweetly and said, "Oh yes, we certainly have."

There was a big cardboard check resting on an easel underneath the lights. *Pay to the order of Jessie Peacock,* it read. *$5,000,000.* Jessie counted the zeroes. Six of them.

Then Jessie heard applause. The governor had entered the rotunda. He came forward to shake Jessie and Asa's hands. The flashbulbs popped. Jessie was dazed. She was weakening, Asa could tell. He put his hand on her elbow to steady her.

"Remember your testimony," he whispered in her ear.

They stood in front of the check. The governor spoke, then directed Jessie to come to the microphone, which she did. She stood upright and stared into the lights. The flashbulbs popped. She opened her mouth and began to speak.

"I despise the lottery. It preys on the ignorant. It brings out the worst in people, not the best. It encourages sloth and envy and all that I deplore. Therefore, I cannot in good conscience accept this money."

She said it from memory. She'd practiced in front of the mirror the night before. She turned and smiled at the governor, who looked rather queasy.

He said, "You can't do that."

She said, "Watch me!"

Then she took the check from the easel and tore it in half. It was thick cardboard, but she was a strong Quaker woman. It ripped right down the middle.

Jessie hadn't planned on tearing the check, but the idea came to her during her speech, and it seemed a good one. It felt like the thing to do. A dramatic statement. A testimony.

She was right. It played on all the television stations that evening.

Bob Miles Jr. couldn't have been happier. Finally, something to write about. This was better than a murder.

"Peacock Kills Goose That Laid Golden Egg," read the headline. It was a clever headline. Even Jessie thought so. She and Asa bought three extra copies to mail to their children.

Jessie told Asa, "I didn't even think about the kids. I hope they're not upset with us."

But they weren't. They were proud. To Jessie, that was better than having five million dollars, having your children proud of you. It's a good thing when parents are proud of their children, but it's especially fine when children take pride in their parents.

The state sent her a check anyway, along with a letter saying Jessie had to cash it—it was the law.

She wrote *I refuse to accept this money* across the face of the check and mailed it back.

A man from the lottery came to see her. He said when Jessie bought the ticket, she accepted certain obligations to take the money.

She said, "I didn't buy the ticket. It was given to me."

He said her refusing to take the money made the lottery look bad.

"That's precisely what I'd hoped," she told him, then showed him the door.

*T*his has never happened before. They're saying it might end up in court. Jessie's ready to go. She's never felt this alive. It's a wonderful thing to have a testimony.

They've been talking about it down at the Coffee Cup. Those old men sit at the liar's table underneath the swordfish and talk about what they'd have done with five million dollars. Dumb things. They want to open bait shops. They want to corner the worm market.

I'm glad I didn't win. I'd have bought my mother a dishwasher and she and my father wouldn't have stood side by side anymore—she washing, he drying and putting away. They'd have stopped looking out the kitchen window at the finches on the feeder. They'd have been the poorer for it.

Those old men sit down at the Coffee Cup wishing they'd hit it big. What they don't realize is that they already have. If you can go home to someone who loves you, if your children are proud of you, if you can keep your integrity, you've hit the jackpot. You don't need the state to call your number. It's already been called.

Twenty-three

Legal Grounds

The reason for our town's unbroken chain of bliss is that for seventeen years, we had only one lawyer—Owen Stout. With a shortage of lawyers to cultivate hostility, couples who might have divorced stayed married and resolved their conflicts. Persons inclined to sue, having no lawyer to further their claim, settled their contentions peaceably. Besides, it is against our religion to sue each other, so we don't hire lawyers, we just stop talking to one another. This caused the lawyers to stay away in droves.

So Owen Stout lived in a regular house on a regular street, but was dreaming of a bigger home after Jessie Peacock won five million dollars in the lottery. He was going to charge her 10 percent of the winnings to manage her affairs, except Jessie declined the money, saying the lottery was immoral. Owen was glad Jessie was a woman of virtue; he just wished she'd put off virtue until he had his 10 percent.

Owen had made his peace with his modest income. What annoyed him was walking into the Coffee Cup for lunch and having to listen to the lawyer jokes. Ernie Matthews, who spent eight years in high school, would spy Owen and start in with his lawyer jokes, and people would laugh as if Ernie were a genius.

There would be Ernie, sitting at the counter, blowing into his hands.

"Man, it's cold out there," he'd say. "It's so cold, I just saw a lawyer with his hands in his own pockets."

The old men at the liar's table under the swordfish would hoot. They thought Ernie was hysterical.

Thus encouraged, Ernie would tell another.

He'd say, "What does a lawyer use for birth control?"

The old men would think about that, then one of them would ask, "I don't know. What does a lawyer use for birth control?"

Ernie would answer, "His personality."

They thought that was hilarious. They'd pound the table and snort.

Owen would just smile and eat his eggs, and maybe reach over and slap Ernie's back and say, "That's real funny, Ernie. You're pretty clever." All the while thinking to himself, You moron. What do you know?

Which, of course, he couldn't say out loud. He could think it, but he couldn't say it. When you're a public figure in a small town, you have to treat people with dignity, even Ernie Matthews.

I t was a lonely feeling being the only lawyer in town, the sole target of lawyer jokes. So when Owen received a letter in early February from a Ms. Haroldeena Morrison, informing him of her desire to move to Harmony and practice law with Owen, he was relieved that the burden of ridicule would finally be shared.

He had been to the Coffee Cup. When he returned to his office, the letter was laying on his floor, underneath the mail slot. He read the return address. Ms. Haroldeena Morrison. He repeated her name to himself. Haroldeena Morrison…Haroldeena Morrison…Then her name registered. Haroldeena Morrison was the only grandchild of Harold and Mabel Morrison. Her father had named her Haroldeena for his father, over the strong objections of his wife.

Owen Stout remembered the widow Mabel Morrison talking about Haroldeena. She'd graduated from law school, the letter said, and had passed the bar and was looking for a job. She'd be in town the next day and wondered if she could meet with him.

She arrived at Owen's office the next day, just before lunch. Owen was shocked. She didn't look like a Haroldeena. She was exquisite, the prettiest woman he'd ever seen in Harmony, prettier even than the Sausage Queens. Haroldeena Morrison didn't look like she'd eaten many sausages. She looked very…womanly. Owen Stout knew he couldn't give her a job. Before she'd even said a word he knew he couldn't hire her, for fear of subjecting his wife to the gossip and speculation.

Oh, Haroldeena Morrison was ravishing. She reached across the desk and shook his hand. Her hand lingered in his. Owen Stout began to sweat. He'd never touched a lovelier hand. He couldn't bear the temptation.

"Welcome to Harmony, Haroldeena," Owen said.

"Thank you," she said. "But please call me Deena."

Owen rose from his chair and smiled and said brightly, "Lunch?" And he took her to the Coffee Cup, whose atmosphere would stifle any romantic urgings.

They walked around the corner to the Coffee Cup. Owen pushed open the door. The bell tinkled. Everyone looked up. They stared at Deena. What was this? Who was this beautiful creature? They wanted to ask, but it wouldn't have been polite. What was she doing with Owen? The speculation began in earnest.

Ernie Matthews was seated at the counter reading a book.

Owen said, "Hello, Ernie. What you reading?"

Ernie said, "Well, it's a book about two ex-convicts. One of them studies to become a lawyer, and the other decides to go straight."

Ernie erupted in laughter. The old men hooted and pounded the table.

"Aren't you the clever one," Owen said, slapping Ernie on the back.

Owen and Deena sat in a booth by the front window. It was there Owen told her he couldn't hire her, that there wasn't enough business.

"Heck, I can't even afford a secretary," he told her. "Why don't you practice in the city? You seem like a smart person. You could make a good living up there."

Deena talked about how when she was little, she would come to Harmony to visit her grandparents, Harold and Mabel Morrison. She remembered them taking her to the soda fountain at the Rexall. Remembered sleeping in her Grandma's bed with the windows up, listening to the crickets. She was tired of the city. Tired of the noise and the haste and the crime.

She said, "I want to live here. I want to meet a nice man and get married and have children and be a lawyer in this town."

Owen looked at Ernie Matthews, who was probing his ear with his finger.

"Your choice of suitors," Owen told Deena, "will be drastically limited."

*A*gainst Owen's counsel, Deena Morrison moved to Harmony. Her Grandmother Mabel let her use the old Morrison's Menswear building. She had a sign made, *Deena Morrison, Attorney-at-Law*, and hired Ernie Matthews to paint the inside, a monumentally stupid blunder. Ernie made jokes the whole time, and whenever Deena looked his direction, he'd be staring at her, his finger in his ear. He thought Deena had hired him because she had a crush on him. He began wearing Old Spice aftershave. His pants came to just beneath his gut. He'd bend over to pour paint, his pants would slip, and she'd see more of him than she really wanted to. It discouraged her, listening to his lawyer jokes and catching glimpses of his pale backside.

People began to drop hints about her dating Ernie.

"He's a catch," they'd tell her. "Owns his own truck and paints real good."

Deena told her grandmother, "I'm going to die a lonely old woman, with no one to mourn my passing. I'll be like one of those women you read about in the paper who they find a month after she's died. I'll die all alone in a house full of cats."

She came to church at Harmony Friends Meeting, hoping to meet someone. The women of the Mary and Martha class invited her to Sunday school. They read from the book of Proverbs about being good wives.

Fern Hampton hinted that Deena was too picky. "There never was a horse that you couldn't find a bush to tie it to," she told Deena.

Great, thought Deena. Now I'm a horse.

The law practice wasn't working out. Deena was getting cynical. She complained to her grandmother that people in Harmony didn't want women working outside the home unless they were teaching kids or pouring coffee. Then, if they marry, they're to do the proper thing and quit.

One nasty, early spring Sunday afternoon, Deena drove to the city to a coffee shop. It was no ordinary coffee shop. It had brick walls and antique tables with linen tablecloths. There were bookshelves full of books with a fireplace along the back wall. She sat near the fire and read Walt Whitman's *Leaves of Grass* and felt sophisticated. She liked Harmony, but the only copy of *Leaves of Grass* was in the library and hadn't been checked out since 1973 when Dale Hinshaw mistook it for a book on lawn maintenance.

Deena sat there, listening to the pleasant murmur of conversation, waiting for the server and marveling at this oasis of civility. She looked out the window at the rain and the swelling buds on the trees and thought of the promise they held. I want a new life, she thought. Sitting there, in all that civility, it occurred to her that she didn't really want to be a lawyer after all. She'd have to move to the city, where the practice of law was nothing but an organized battle for money. A fiscal brawl. She wanted no part of it.

She wanted to open a coffee shop, just like this one, in Harmony. An oasis of civility. Why not? She had the building. She'd made coffee before. She grew excited thinking of it. She fished a notebook from her purse and began writing her ideas.

There was a young man waiting on tables wearing a T-shirt which read, *They'll never take me alive.* His left eyebrow was pierced with a gold ring. It made Deena queasy to look at him.

She wrote in her notebook, "Do not hire anyone with a pierced eyebrow."

The young man came to her table and asked, "Whad'll you have?"

There were twenty-six flavors of coffee. Deena couldn't decide. The man rolled his eyes, which caused his eyebrow ring to bob up and down. Deena's stomach rolled.

She peered at the menu. She could make out the words *crisp brightness* and *full body* and *Trinidad Peaberry Blend* and *Country Morning Blend.*

She decided on the Country Morning Blend. It tasted pretty good. It was a little like bacon and eggs, with buttered toast on the side.

Deena didn't think she could start with twenty-six flavors. That was a bit ambitious. She'd start with one flavor and go from there. She'd call it "Harmony Blend." It would be just like the town—mostly plain with a few nuts thrown in. She wrote that in her notebook.

She finished her coffee and drove back to Harmony, to her grandmother's house. They sat in the kitchen and Deena told her grandmother her idea.

"A coffee shop, Grandma!" she told her. "A coffee shop that doesn't smell like stale grease and cigarettes, no old men cackling at lawyer jokes, where the waitress won't chew gum and say, 'Whad'll you have?' but will instead glide up to your table and smile and say, 'How may I help you?' An oasis of civility!"

Mabel Morrison clapped her hands. "Haroldeena, that's a wondrous thought," she declared. "Can I help?"

So they sat, grandmother and granddaughter, through the evening, plotting and planning. They began writing down everything they knew about coffee. They knew there was coffee with caffeine, which was served in a brown pot, and coffee without caffeine, which was served in an orange pot. They knew if you forgot and left the coffeepot turned on all day, the coffee would burn and turn hard.

Deena wrote that in her notebook. *Don't forget to turn off coffeepot at end of day.*

*I*t took Deena and Mabel two months to get the coffee shop ready. They ripped off the paneling down to the old bricks and sanded the wood floors. They put a fireplace on the back wall. On Sundays they went to antique shops and bought tables and chairs. They went up to Mabel's attic and hauled down the big red goose from the International Shoe Company of St. Louis.

Mabel said, "It belongs in that building. It's been there forty-two years. It doesn't belong in my attic. You watch, Haroldeena, people will come in just to see that goose."

They set the red goose above the coffeepots; then to the right of the goose hung Deena's law diploma, along with a sign which read:

No lawyer jokes permitted.
Violators will be fined five dollars.

She put a jar next to the cash register for the fines.

Her grandmother asked, "Deena, honey, what are we going to name our coffee shop? We need a name."

Deena said, "Grandma, I've been thinking about it. I think we ought to call it 'Legal Grounds.'"

Mabel smiled. "I like it," she said. So the sign painter from the city came and took down the *Deena Morrison, Attorney-at-Law* sign and hung up the *Legal Grounds Coffee Shop* sign.

Deena and Mabel opened the Legal Grounds Coffee Shop on a Saturday morning. By ten o'clock all the tables were full. Everyone in town who couldn't abide the stale grease and cackling old men of the Coffee Cup came to dwell in this oasis of civility. The window was steamy. People were drinking their cups of Harmony Blend. It was delicious—a miracle in a mug. They drank their miracle and talked about important things, and no one made fun of them.

They talked about the rise of political liberalism in Europe and the growing trade imbalance. Deena read a poem from *Leaves of Grass*. Then they sipped their coffee, and listened to Luciano Pavarotti singing "Nessun Dorma" from the opera, *Turandot*. All this culture and beauty in our town, which had been hidden for fear of what others might think, was now allowed to blossom.

At least until ten-thirty. That's when Ernie Matthews clomped in and sat at a table, backward in a chair, his elbows resting on the chair's back. "How can you tell when a lawyer is lying?" he asked in a loud voice.

The room fell quiet. People turned to stare. Mistaking their attention for interest, Ernie said, "When her lips are moving!" He cackled and slapped the table.

He looked at Deena and grinned. He'd read somewhere that women like a man with a sense of humor.

But Deena didn't laugh. Nor did anyone else. They just stared at him.

Deena pointed to the sign next to the goose: *No lawyer jokes permitted. Violators will be fined five dollars.*

Ernie said, "That's ridiculous. I ain't paying five dollars. Whoever heard of such a thing? I ain't paying that."

"Ernie, you'll have to pay five dollars or leave," Deena said. She said it politely and smiled.

Ernie paid the five dollars. He wasn't happy, but he paid it. He crammed it in the jar, then drank his coffee and stomped out and didn't come back for two weeks.

Things were going good for Deena. People would sit in the Legal Grounds and drink their Harmony Blend and talk about things that mattered. Three or four times a day someone would spy her diploma next to the red goose and ask Deena's advice on their legal matters. That's when she came up with the idea of hanging up another sign which read:

Two questions for ten dollars.

You could ask Deena any two questions for ten dollars.

That next Saturday Ernie Matthews lumbered in and read the sign and said, "Two questions for ten dollars. Isn't that a bit steep?"

Deena said, "I don't think so. Now what's your second question?"

She does a big business with the eligible farmers. They come there just to see her. She's so pretty. They watch as she works her way from table to table, pouring coffee and smiling at people. Oh, that smile. On days when it's raining and they can't work the fields, they drive into town to gaze at her. Deena-gazing. They sip their coffee and fall in love to the strains of Pavarotti. They imagine what it might be like to marry her. The thought overwhelms. They switch to decaf to steady their nerves. Some days she'll read poetry. They imagine, as she recites a particularly lovely phrase, that she is directing the verse at them.

On some evenings, if his neighbor comes early to watch the children, Wayne Fleming will stop by the Legal Grounds on his way to work at the Kroger. His wife had run off, had left him and the children, and had never come back. Wayne sits there amid the civility and for a moment, while gazing at Deena, is transported beyond his tired trailer and broken life. He wonders what it would be like to marry Deena.

She'd be such a fine mother to my children, he thinks. He imagines she is drawn to him. When he walks to the counter to pay for the coffee, she waves him away with a small brush of her hand. She smiles, he smiles. Such a decent woman, he thinks.

He loves her. He will never tell her that for fear she would not return his sentiments. But late at night, when the Kroger is quiet and he is sweeping the floors, Wayne thinks of her and it fills his heart.

She's a wonderful woman, he thinks. She would be so good for my children. I would love her so much.

He prays about it. "Dear sweet Lord, cause her to love me." He prays that prayer over and over, aisle after aisle.

Then his shift is over and he climbs into his truck and goes back to his trailer, strengthened for the day.

Love, even that love which is imagined, is sometimes all we have to get us through.

Twenty-four

The Shroud of Harmony

The Friendly Women's Circle was begun in 1898, to "Uplift and Preserve All That Is Magnificent." But magnificence being in short supply in Harmony, they moved on to other things. Time has not improved our situation. Drive into our town from the east and see Harvey Muldock's car dealership with its flags and its bright orange signs, and magnificence is not the word that comes to mind. So while they started out with a high purpose, to uplift and preserve all that is magnificent, they worked their way down the ladder fairly quickly.

Their main goal these days is to raise money for Brother Norman's shoe ministry to the Choctaw Indians. Their aim is to never see a shoeless Choctaw, which they've accomplished.

The Friendly Women's Circle's main fundraiser since 1964 has been the Chicken Noodle Dinner, which is held every September during Harmony's annual Corn and Sausage Days. But in 1974, Fern Hampton, then president of the Circle, decided the women needed to diversify their business interests.

"If it rains the weekend of Corn and Sausage Days, we're sunk," she told the Circle. "We need to diversify."

They would talk about it on Tuesday mornings while they rolled out noodles. They would talk about venture capital and marketing strategies.

Mrs. Dale Hinshaw told how she and Dale had been thinking it over and they thought the Friendly Women's Circle could sponsor a demolition derby in the church parking lot. She told how they had them up in the city and people turned out in droves.

Jessie Peacock suggested holding a Spam festival. She had saved the proofs of purchase from three cans of Spam and sent them in for a book of Spam recipes, which she had been trying out on Asa. Spam tacos, Spamburgers, and their favorite Spam dish of all, Spam kabobs.

She said, "We could call it Spam Jam. People would come from all over. They do one up in Minnesota and twenty thousand people show up. We could do one here. No reason we couldn't."

Fern said, "Well, it's something to think about, I guess. Any other ideas?"

"Maybe we could sell our noodles," Miriam Hodge suggested. "The Amish women do that. They sell them on street corners. Sell them right from their buggies. We could do that."

"That might be dangerous," Fern said. "Those Amish women take their noodles seriously. We start selling noodles on their turf and we could end up in an early grave. I don't want a noodle war."

My grandmother was thinking hard, frowning. Then she brightened. "Maybe we could sell a quilt. We take those three months off in the winter and don't make noodles. Maybe we could use that time to stitch a quilt that we could raffle off at the Chicken Noodle Dinner."

Fern said, "I like that idea. We could do one quilt a year. Some of those quilts sell for hundreds of dollars. We could do that. That would buy a lot of shoes."

S o that's what they've done every year since 1974. They meet every Tuesday morning at nine o'clock. They ease down the stairs, hunker down at the quilting frame, and stitch for three solid hours. Every January, February, and March.

Their husbands want to spend the winter in Florida and play golf, but these women wouldn't dream of it. There's work to be done. Quilts to be made. Indians to be shod. How can you think of golf when there are shoeless Indians running around? Now is not the time for play; now is the time for duty; now is the time to uplift and preserve all that is magnificent.

They have it down pat. They assemble at nine A.M., then at ten-thirty, take a fifteen minute break. Fern times them. They drink coffee, way across the room, over by the freezer. Fern won't allow them near the quilt with coffee. Then she makes them wash their hands, then they're right back at it—uplifting and preserving all that is magnificent.

My first year as their pastor was the twenty-fifth anniversary of the Friendly Women's Circle quilt sale. It was also Fern's turn to be president again. It being an anniversary year, Fern and the ladies were especially concerned about magnificence.

Way back in October, Fern called the Circle together.

"We want this one to shimmer," Fern told the ladies. "Fifty years from now, we want people to think back on this quilt and quiver. Let's aim for the heavens."

They spent the next three months drawing sketches. No store-bought pattern for this quilt. The Lord Himself would provide the pattern. They set aside a morning to pray over the quilting frame. They laid their hands on it and began to pray. Fern started to shake.

"It's a sign," she told them. "God has great things in store for this quilt. I can feel it."

They began stitching in January. Worked all the way through

February and into March. On the last week of March, they came to the basement every day but Sunday.

By that time, Fern had dispensed with the coffee drinking altogether. She told them, "Caffeine makes your hands shake. It'll cause crooked stitches. No more coffee."

They finished the last week of March.

That quilt was magnificent. It shimmered. They carried it up from the basement and hung it from the wall at the front of the meeting room, in back of the pulpit. It pulsed with beauty.

People walked into worship talking about sciatica and rheumatism and gas mileage, then saw the quilt hanging there and fell quiet, awestruck. Such magnificence.

I could barely bring myself to preach, for fear my common words would detract from such beauty. I cut it short. They weren't paying attention anyway. They were fixed on the quilt. We settled into silence, waiting for the Lord to speak. Five minutes passed, then ten.

The sun crested the trees and shone right through the windows onto the quilt. It dazzled. People gasped at the beauty.

Then Fern's voice rose from the sixth row. "I see Him," she said. "Look. He's right there. Look at the quilt. He's in the quilt."

*A*ll across the meeting room, people raised their eyes. I heard more gasps. And then I saw Him, dead center in the quilt. A man's face. But not just any man. *The Man.* Jesus. Right there on the quilt. At least it looked like Jesus. Then, just that quick, He was gone.

Fern said, "I knew it. I knew God had something in mind for that quilt. I told you. Didn't I tell you?"

We were so startled we forgot to take the offering. Instead, we brought worship to a close and the elders went to the basement for an emergency meeting.

Dale Hinshaw said, "The Catholics are good with this kind of thing. Let's call the Vatican and get the pope out here. Me and the missus'll put him up at our house on the pullout sofa. He'll know what to do."

"We've got to keep this quiet," Miriam Hodge advised. "Otherwise, this place will get crazy. People will come from all over to see the quilt. We don't want that. We have to keep this quiet."

But it was too late. Fern Hampton had already phoned Bob Miles Jr., who came and took a picture of the quilt and ran a story about it in the *Herald*. "The Shroud of Harmony," read the headline.

The Associated Press picked up the story and within a few days a line of people stretched out the meetinghouse door, down Main Street, past the Coffee Cup. Vinny and Penny Toricelli at the Coffee Cup began using a cookie cutter to shape hamburger patties in the shape of an angel. They served Angel Burger Value Meals: one Angel Burger, Halo Rings—which were actually onion rings—Angel Food Cake, and your choice of beverage for $5.99.

Dale Hinshaw organized the ushers to serve as guards. People stood before the quilt and watched for Jesus. Every now and then, when the sun would crest the trees and shine through the windows onto the quilt, someone would see Him.

One day, when Dale Hinshaw was guarding the quilt, he reached up and touched it and was cured of a head cold.

"My sinuses just opened up," he reported. "I could feel 'em draining."

There was talk of taking the quilt on the road, showing it at other Quaker meetings. Maybe charging admission and using the money to buy shoes for the Choctaw Indians.

Fern wouldn't hear of it. "You don't just haul the Lord from place to place. It's unseemly." So the quilt stayed put and the people kept coming.

Then certain items began to disappear from the meetinghouse—hymn books and cardboard fans compliments of the Mackey Funeral Home. Total strangers began chipping away pieces of our pews. They were stripping us clean. Things were getting out of hand.

I took to working at the meetinghouse early in the morning, before the crowds arrived. I came to my office one morning to find Miriam Hodge waiting for me.

She said, "This has gotten out of hand."

I said, "I know. But I don't think we should stop it. It might be from the Lord. We have to be careful."

Miriam said, "Sam, I have something to tell you. I came by one evening when we were finishing up the quilt. I wanted to finish a section. I was by myself. I was drinking my coffee and I spilled it all over the quilt. I took it home and cleaned it as best I could and brought it back the next morning. But Sam, that's not the Lord we've been seeing, that's Maxwell House."

I was struck dumb.

Miriam went on, "We have to tell people. We have to tell Fern. We can't let this go on. It's a fraud. We can't keep this up."

We called Fern on the phone and asked her to come to the meetinghouse, which she did. We told her about Miriam spilling coffee on the quilt.

Fern took it better than we thought. She cried a little, then she sniffed and said, "It's still a beautiful quilt."

"It is that," I told her. "It's pure magnificence. And you can leave it up as long as you wish."

She said, "Just until the Chicken Noodle Dinner. Then we'll raffle it off. It'll buy a lot of shoes." Then she left.

I called Bob Miles Jr. and told him it wasn't Jesus, it was Maxwell

House. He ran the correction that very week. The lines dwindled. Dale Hinshaw dismissed the guards, though he still swore he'd been cured of a head cold. Things got back to normal.

*T*he Monday before Easter, I woke up early and went and sat in the fifth row and looked up at the quilt. A small part of me wished it had been Him. I found a certain joy in watching people step carefully into the meetinghouse, their hands clasped, seeking out the divine. Witnessing such raw hope, such sure belief, was a quiet thrill.

But in my more thoughtful moments, I'm glad it wasn't Jesus. It troubled me that folks would drive three hundred miles to see Christ in a quilt, but wouldn't walk next door to see Him in their neighbor.

I don't think we ought to look for Christ in a quilt. I think we ought to look for Christ in the poor, in the common, in the lady who rings up our groceries, in the man who mops the grocery floor, in the kid who delivers our pizza.

I talked about it in my Easter message. I told how we always look for Christ amid magnificence. But that Christ has a history of showing up amid the unlovely. Born in a dirty stall. Crowned with thorns. Died gasping on a shameful cross atop a jagged rise.

We don't need to be beautiful for Christ to take us in. He is equally at home when we're broken-down and dirty. It's like George Herbert wrote:

> *And here in dust and dirt, O here,*
> *The lilies of God's love appear.*

We think magnificence is in short supply, that dust and dirt choke out the lilies. But that's not true and never was. Lilies may root in dirt, but they reach for heaven—and in the reaching, reveal their magnificence.

ACKNOWLEDGMENTS

This book could not have been written without the support and encouragement of many fine people.

Many thanks to Don Jacobson's team at Multnomah Publishers. Their servanthearts are a blessing to me.

Dan Benson and Tom Mullen, my editors, follow behind me, fixing my many errors with nary a complaint. Thank you.

I am grateful to my agents—David Leonards and Steven Green. Their conscientious work enables me to put first things first.

Bill and Carolyn Strafford travel far and wide to help me when I speak. My thanks to them.

The caring people of Fairfield Friends Meeting in Camby, Indiana, are a boon to my spirit.

Most of all, my deep love to my family—Joan, Spencer, and Sam, who fill my life with joy.

In addition to writing, Philip Gulley also enjoys the ministry of speaking. If you would like more information, please contact:

David Leonards

3612 North Washington Boulevard

Indianapolis, Indiana 46205-3592

317-926-7566

ieb@prodigy.net

If you would like to correspond directly with Philip Gulley, please send mail to:

Philip Gulley

c/o Multnomah Publishers

P.O. Box 1720

Sisters, Oregon 97759

Could you use a little more Harmony in your life? Visit the *Home to Harmony* Web site:

www.hometoharmony.com

More life-changing books
by Philip Gulley

Hometown Tales takes you back home with grace-filled stories that unforgettably illustrate the fruit of the Spirit. You'll be inspired to grow spiritually and discover lasting hope in a hope-less world.

ISBN 1-57673-276-2 HD

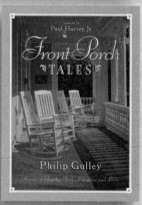

Filled with warm, inspirational stories about the values you want to pass on to future generations, **Front Porch Tales** lifts spirits and helps you gain new perspective on what is important.

ISBN 1-57673-123-5 HD

Through humor and story, **For Everything a Season** identifies and celebrates God's refreshing grace in our everyday moments. It heightens our awareness of God's unfolding love for creation and offers hope to those mired in a culture of despair.

ISBN 1-57673-404-8 HD